CREATE THE BEST PLACE

to keep your entire collection

■

Designed with widely available services and materials

■

Easy-to-follow diagrams and illustrations

■

Engages creativity and imagination

3/10
LEVEL OF DIFFICULTY
Suitable for all skill and experience levels

45
NUMBER OF PARTS
Does not require the purchase of additional parts

60
NUMBER OF CELLS
Compatible with 1/64 scale collectible models

An attractive and functional interior solution

Reduces clutter and keeps toys organized

Easy to extend for growing collections

YOFFE.STUDIO - INSPIRING PROJECTS STEP BY STEP

TOY CARS STORAGE SHELF

DIY MANUAL

CNC & scroll saw woodworking project

Model: V60

MARK YOFFE JR.

CONTENTS

INSTEAD OF INTRODUCTION 9

PART 1
HOW TO USE THIS MANUAL 11

PART 2
WHAT YOU WILL NEED 13

PART 3
PRODUCT SPECIFICATION 15

PART 4
LIST OF PARTS 17

PART 5
MAKING PARTS 19

PART 6
PRE-ASSEMBLING AND ADJUSTMENT 25

PART 7
FINAL ASSEMBLING 35

PART 8
PAINTING AND DRYING 51

INSTEAD OF INTRODUCTION

Welcome to the world of Yoffe.studio, a place where creativity knows no bounds, and everyone is welcome. This book is suitable for all levels of experience and skill. Whether you are a professional who is equipped with all the necessary tools, someone who enjoys assembling pre-made components, or even if you prefer to outsource the entire process and simply get the final result.

This manual offers an exciting project that involves not only applying a variety of skills, but also use of technology. From simple woodworking techniques to an introduction to high-tech CNC equipment, you will find a project that will keep you interested from start to finish.

For those who have children this project can be an opportunity to spend great time and create not just children's craft, but a real, high-quality, and useful addition to the interior. Besides making something beautiful, these hands-on learning experiences encourage kids to be creative, use logic, solve problems and think like engineers.

In addition to the satisfaction of creating something with your own hands, this project can be an original and non-standard gift that will definitely impress your friends and family. Enjoy the process of creativity, learning, and fun that will leave you with more than just beautiful result, but cherished memories and skills that will last a lifetime.

Let's begin!

HOW TO USE THIS MANUAL

READ THROUGH THOROUGHLY

The first step is to read through the entire manual carefully. Take your time to understand the project's scope, required materials, and tools. Pay attention to any safety rules and information signs.

GATHER YOUR TOOLS AND MATERIALS

After understanding the project's requirements, gather all the necessary materials and tools. Ensure that you have everything in place before you begin. This prevents interruptions and keeps your workflow efficient.

FOLLOW THE SEQUENCE

All instructions are organized in a sequential manner. Follow the steps in the order they are presented. Skipping ahead or improvising can lead to errors that may be challenging to fix later. Pay attention for information icons provided with each step. They indicate what materials, tools or actions need to be used or done.

MEASURE TWICE, CUT ONCE

Accuracy and precision are essential to the final result. Double-check your measurements and markings before making any cuts. This simple habit can save you from costly mistakes.

SAFETY FIRST

Prioritize safety throughout your project. Use safety equipment, such as goggles and gloves, as recommended in the manual. Be cautious when operating power tools or using sharp objects, and keep them well-maintained. Please, keep in mind that you are responsible for your kid's safety when working together.

TAKE YOUR TIME

Do not rush through the project. Take your time with each step, ensuring accuracy and quality in your work. Rushing often leads to errors and frustration.

TEST-FIT PARTS

Before final assembling, it is advisable to test-fit components to ensure they align correctly. This can prevent problems that may arise during final assembling.

FINISHING TOUCHES

Follow instructions for finishing, whether it involves sanding, painting, or varnishing. These steps can significantly improve the appearance and lifetime of your product.

WHAT YOU WILL NEED

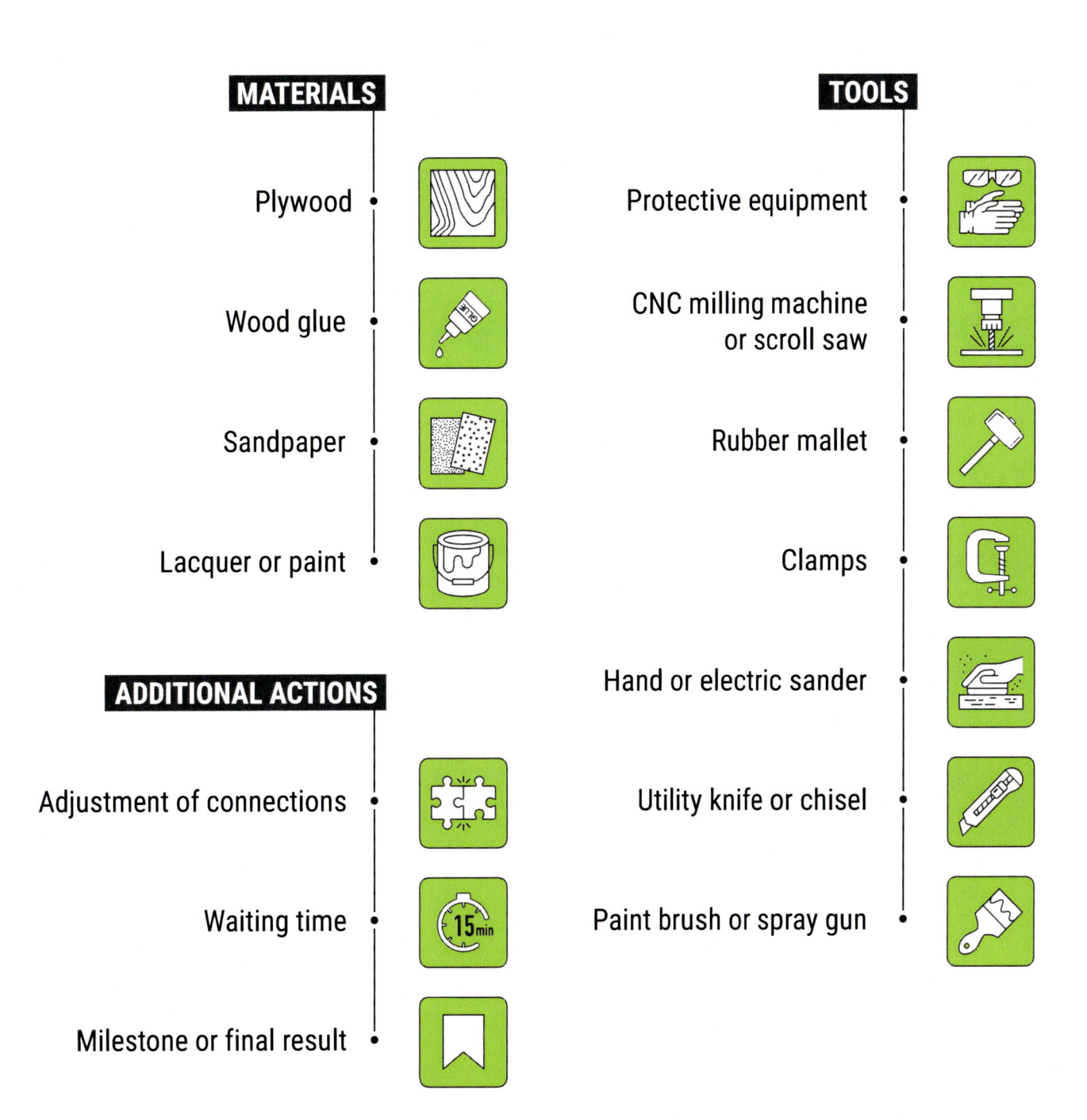

MATERIALS

- Plywood
- Wood glue
- Sandpaper
- Lacquer or paint

ADDITIONAL ACTIONS

- Adjustment of connections
- Waiting time
- Milestone or final result

TOOLS

- Protective equipment
- CNC milling machine or scroll saw
- Rubber mallet
- Clamps
- Hand or electric sander
- Utility knife or chisel
- Paint brush or spray gun

PRODUCT SPECIFICATIONS

PRODUCT SPECIFICATION

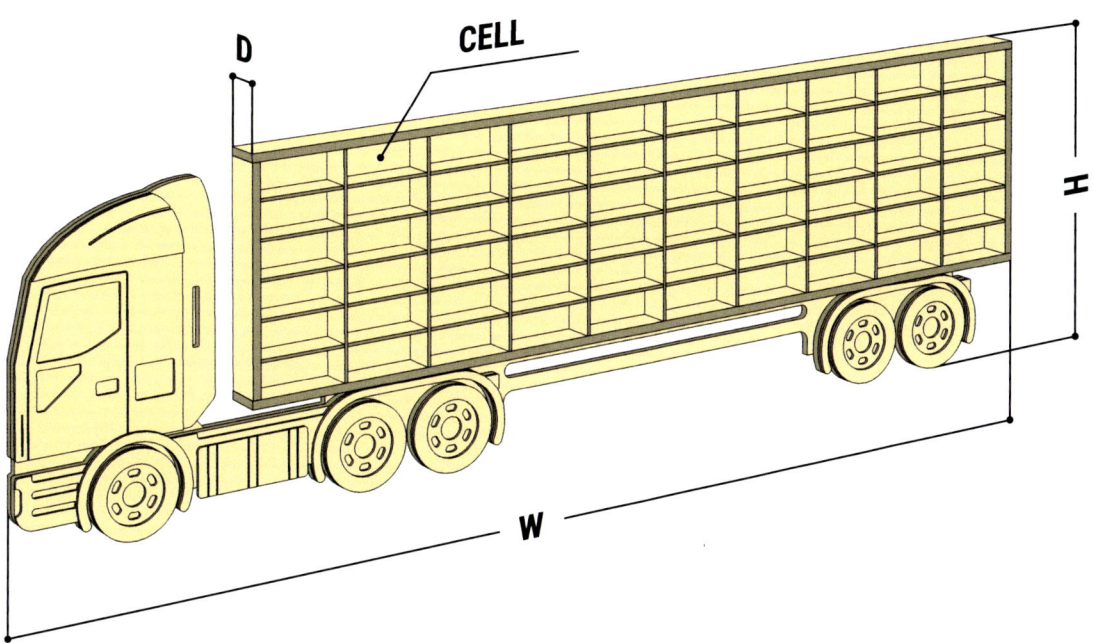

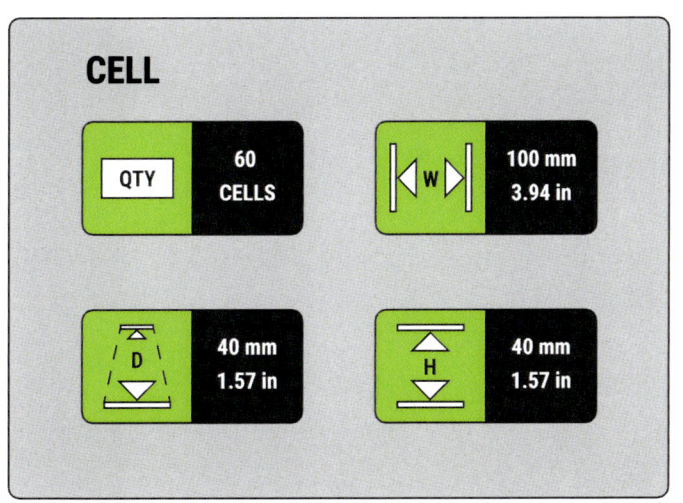

CELL

QTY	60 CELLS
W	100 mm / 3.94 in
D	40 mm / 1.57 in
H	40 mm / 1.57 in

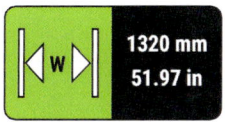
W: 1320 mm / 51.97 in

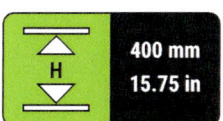
H: 400 mm / 15.75 in

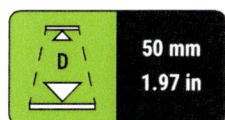
D: 50 mm / 1.97 in

LIST OF PARTS

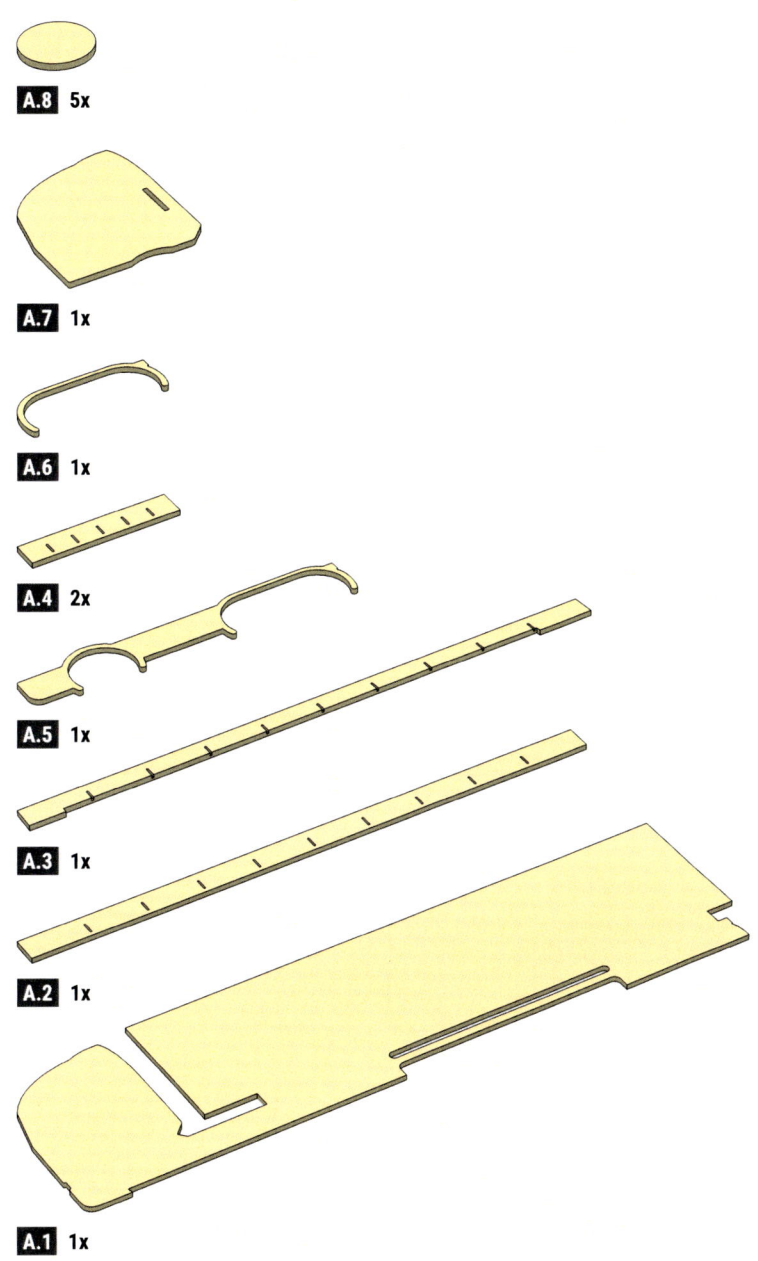

A.8 5x

A.7 1x

A.6 1x

A.4 2x

A.5 1x

A.3 1x

A.2 1x

A.1 1x

LIST OF PARTS

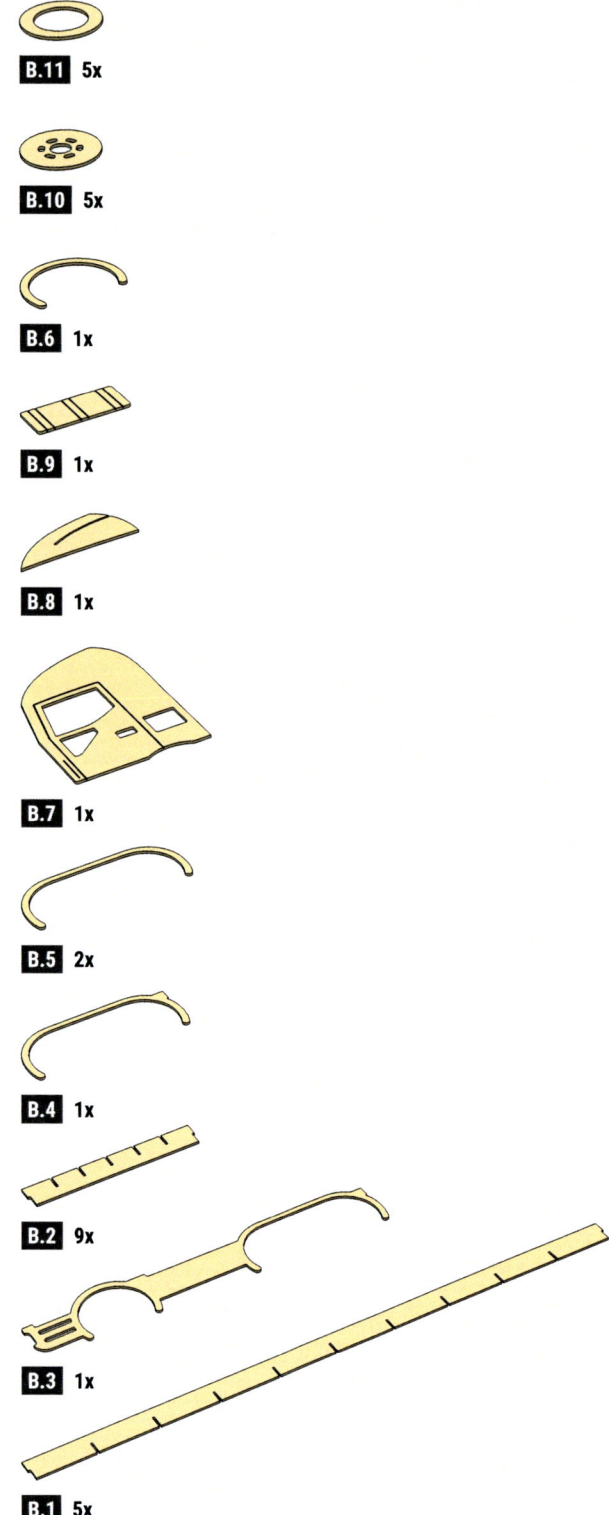

MAKING PARTS

In order to make parts and successfully complete the project it requires the use of a CNC milling machine or scroll saw. However, do not get upset if you have no access to such one. Woodworking services with CNC machine and scroll saw cutting capabilities are well developed and widely available today. That is why I have no doubt that you can easily find several of them in the place you live. Just search for such kind of services nearby.

Also, this section serves as a technical specification guide for producing the required parts. It includes detailed information regarding the quantity and dimensions of materials, recommendations for the most suitable equipment to achieve best results, and specific instructions for manufacturing of some parts.

If you are ordering CNC machine or scroll saw cutting services, be sure to provide the woodworker with this information and additional materials containing vector drawings.

MAKING PARTS

DOWNLOAD OR OPEN VECTOR DRAWINGS

1. **Use your smartphone or tablet to open your device's camera app.**

2. **Scan the QR code below. The camera will recognize it automatically and display a notification or link on your screen.**

3. **Tap on the notification or link to open it. You will be directed to a webpage where you can download the PDF file.**

4. **Once you have downloaded the file, you can access and view the PDF file in your device's PDF reader or import it into other specific app.**

Scan QR code

MAKING PARTS

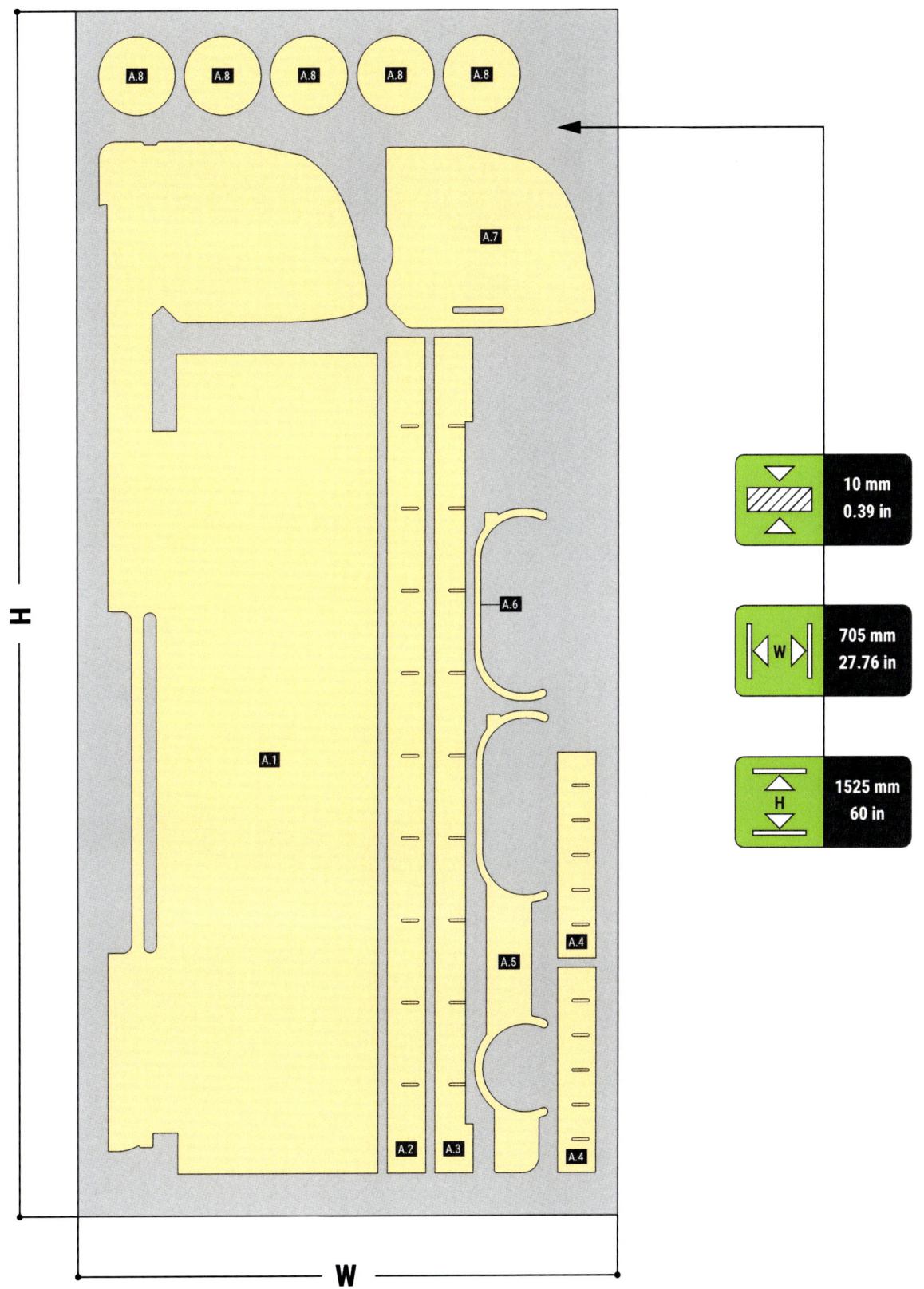

21

MAKING PARTS

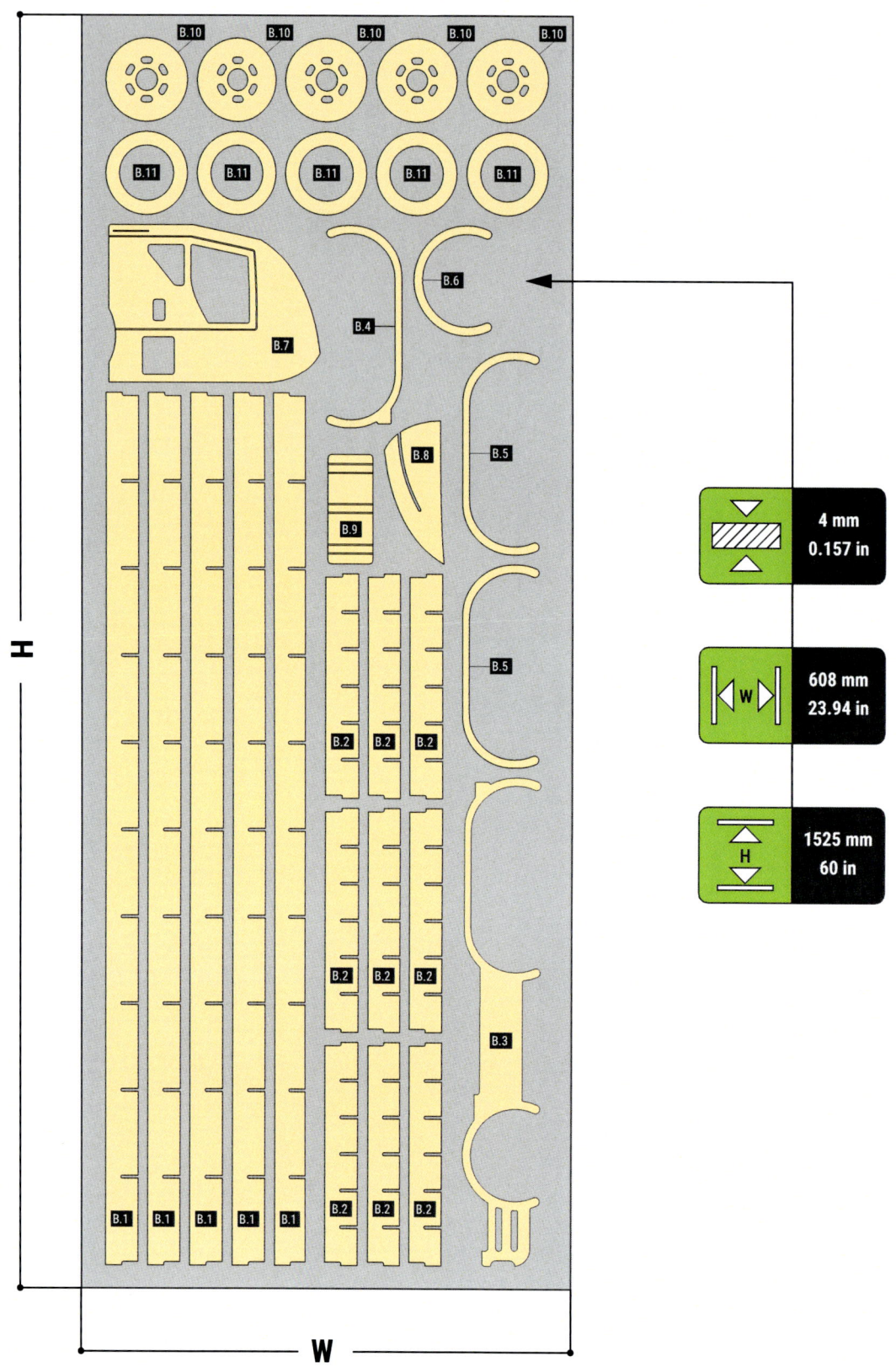

MAKING PARTS

BEST RESULT RECOMENDATION

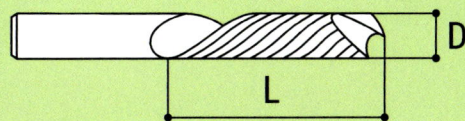

D = 3.175 mm (0.125 in)
L = 12 mm (0.47 in)
Compression (Up Down) End Milling Cutter
with 1 or 2 flutes
Conventional milling

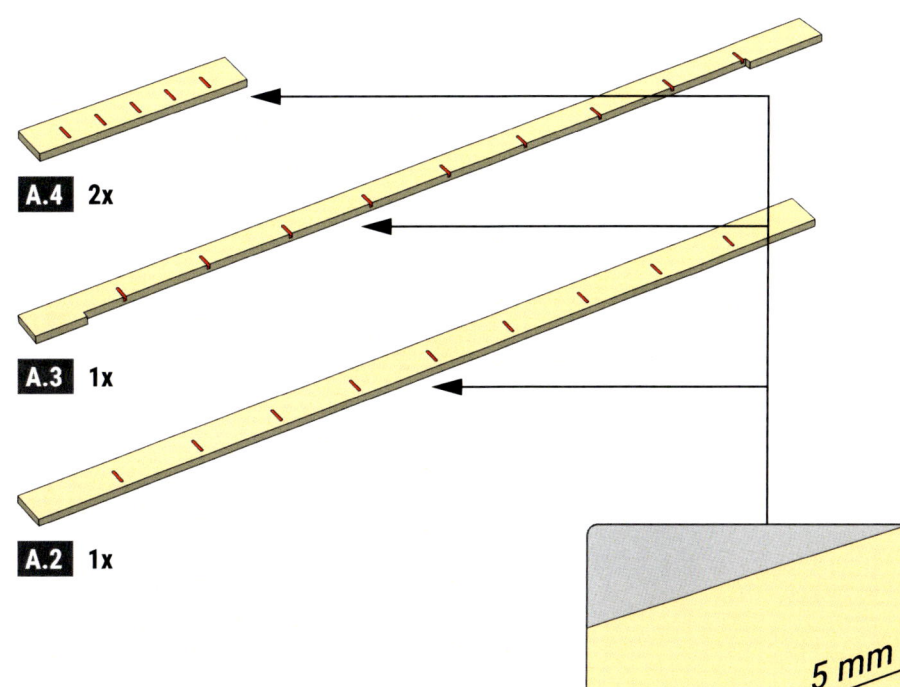

IMPORTANT NOTICE

- If you make these parts with a scroll saw, you will have to use a chisel or hand router to make the mortises.

MAKING PARTS

BEST RESULT RECOMENDATION

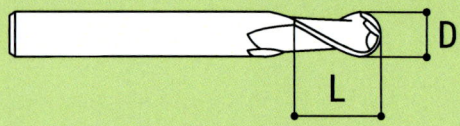

D = 2 mm (0.08 in)
L = 5-10 mm (0.2-0.4 in)
Ball nose Milling Cutter
with straight or spiral flute

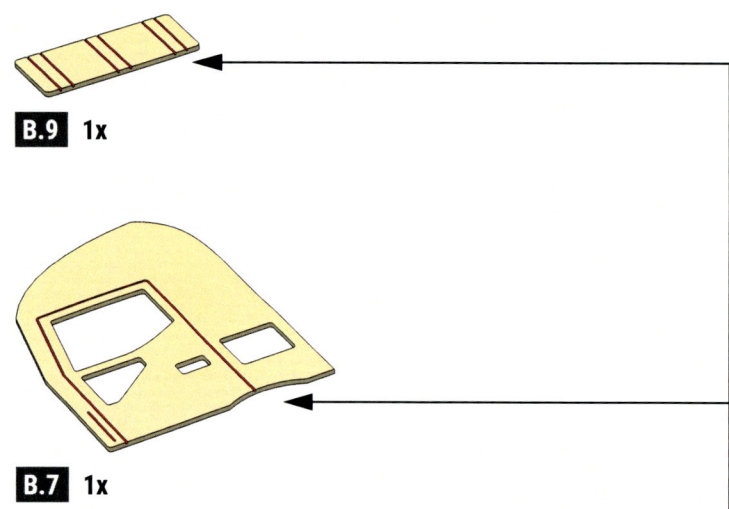

B.9 1x

B.7 1x

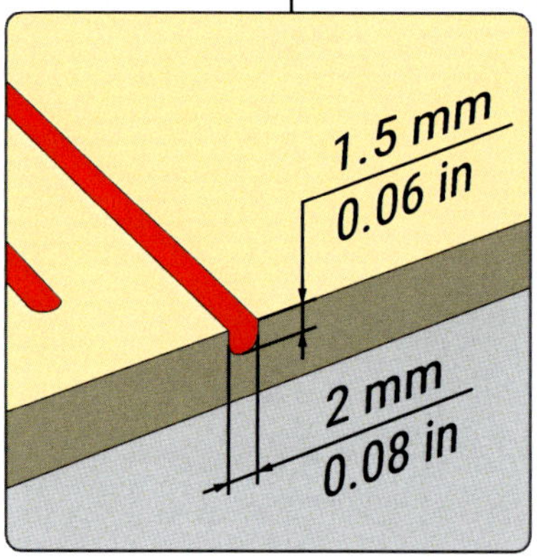

1.5 mm / 0.06 in
2 mm / 0.08 in

IMPORTANT NOTICE

- If you make these parts with a scroll saw, you will have to use a chisel or hand router to make the engravings.

24

PRE-ASSEMBLING AND ADJUSTMENT

PRE-ASSEMBLING AND ADJUSTMENT

IMPORTANT NOTICE

- **This section does not involve the use of glue!**

The primary goal at this part is to ensure that all the parts fit well together before joining and gluing.

Before you start any assembling, you need to thoroughly clean and sand all the parts you have made in the previous section.

All connecting parts should fit tightly but without requiring significant force.

Make sure the edges of all overlaying parts are even and contain no protrusions.

For fitting the parts, we suggest using sandpaper or a file as your main tools. However, if there are significant non-joints, a utility knife can be used as well.

PRE-ASSEMBLING AND ADJUSTMENT

1 THOROUGHLY CLEAN AND SAND ALL THE PARTS

1.1

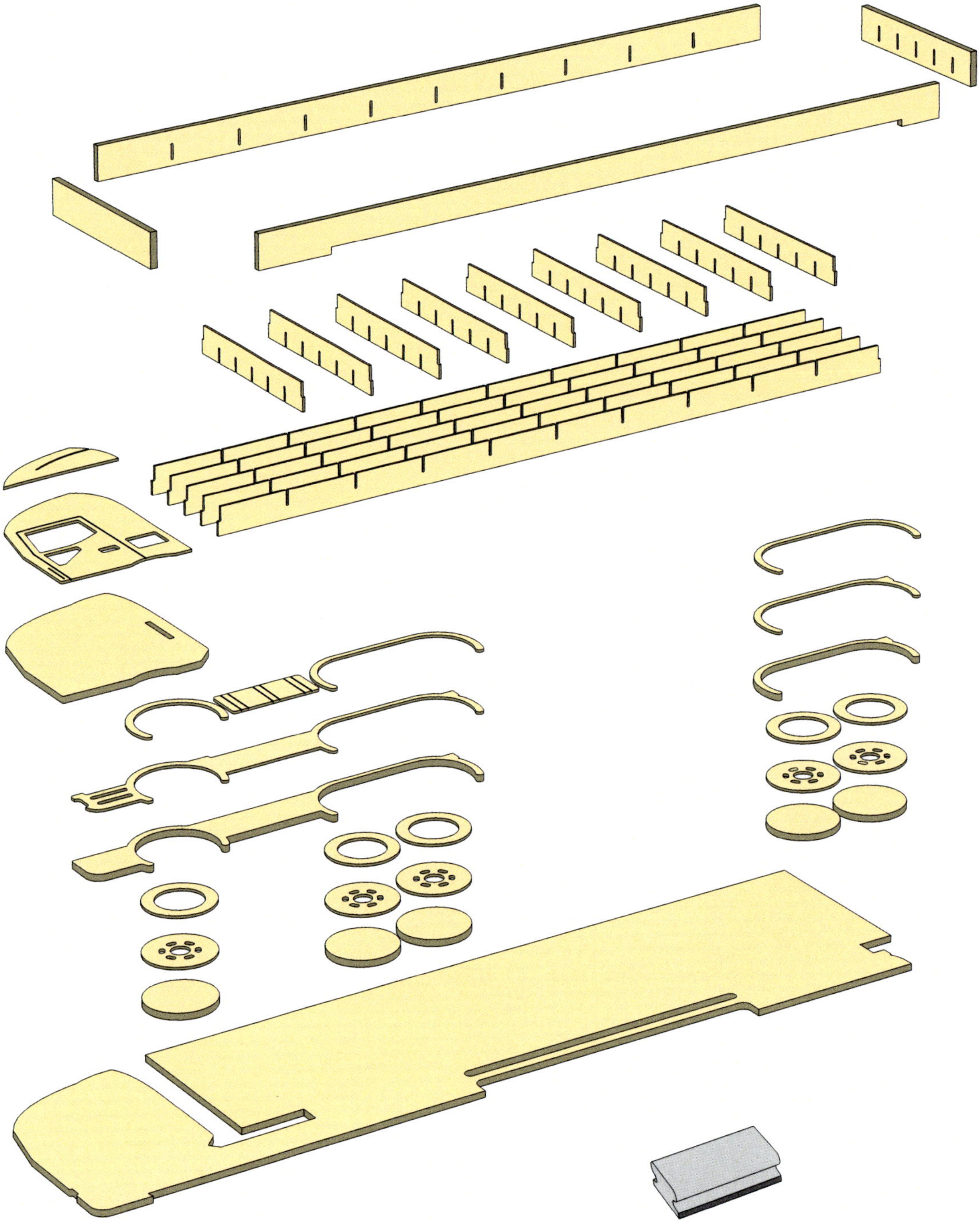

PRE-ASSEMBLING AND ADJUSTMENT

2

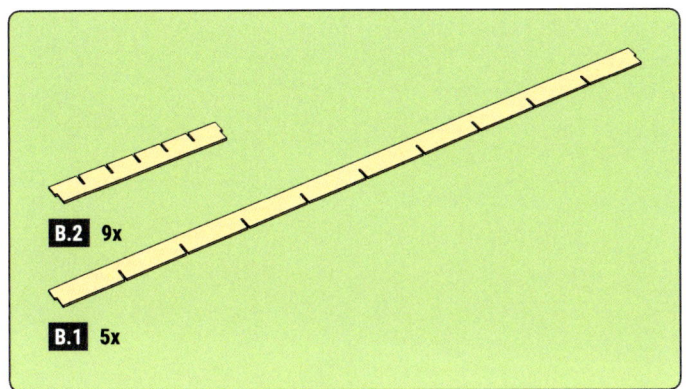

B.2 9x
B.1 5x

2.1

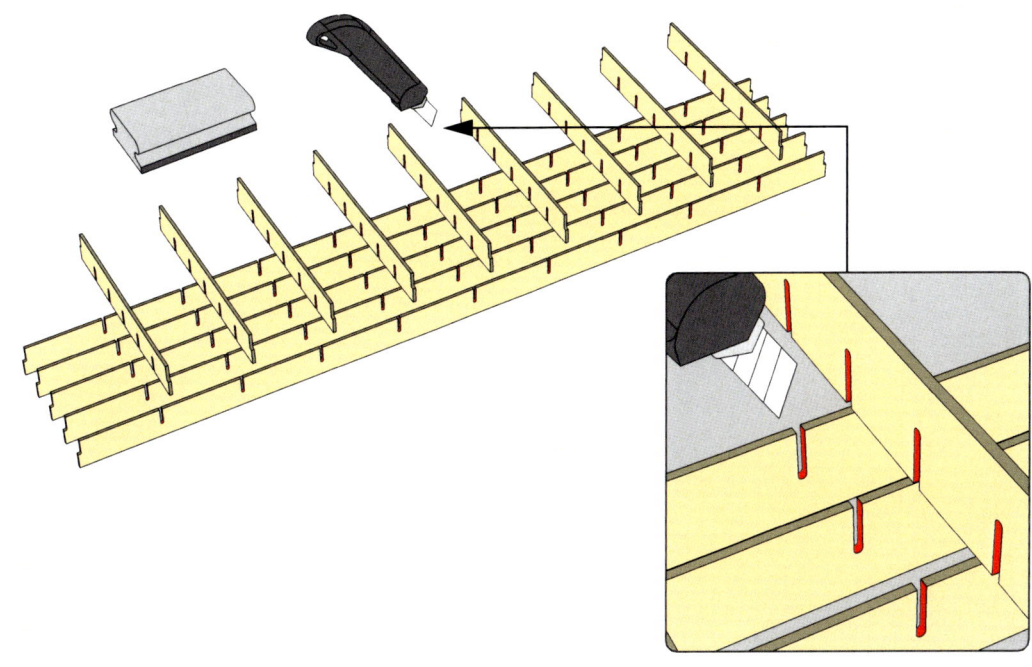

2.2

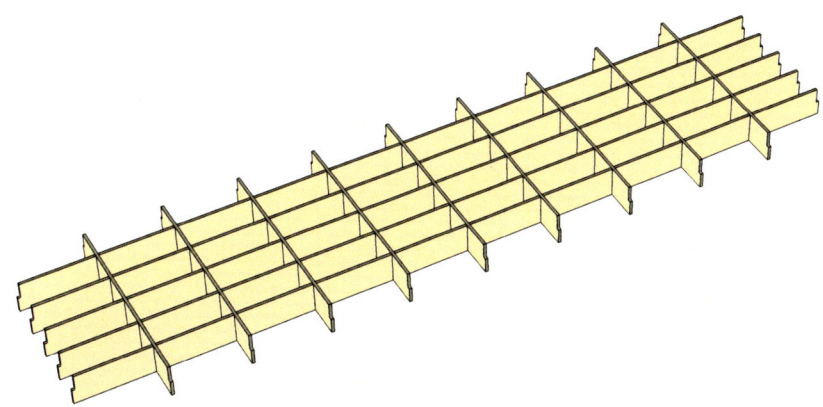

27

PRE-ASSEMBLING AND ADJUSTMENT

3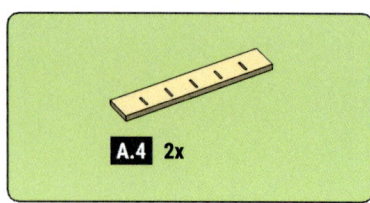

3.1

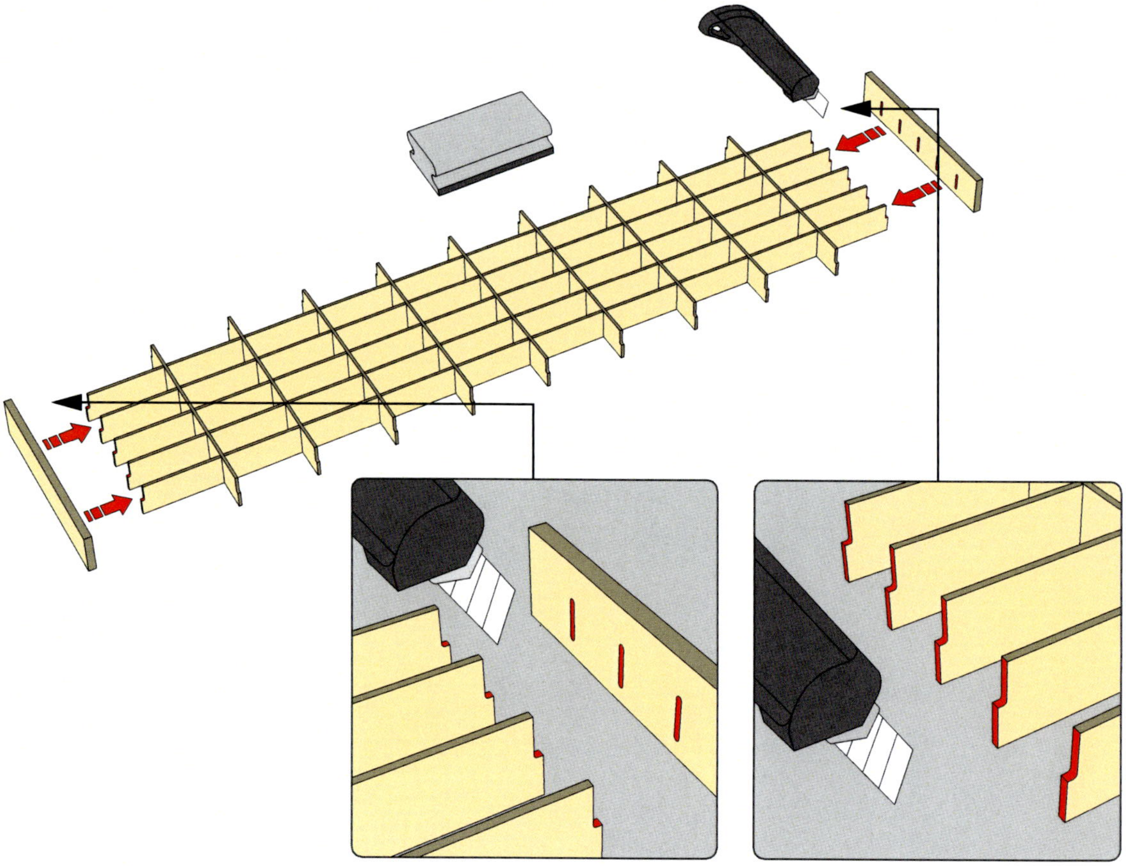

3.2

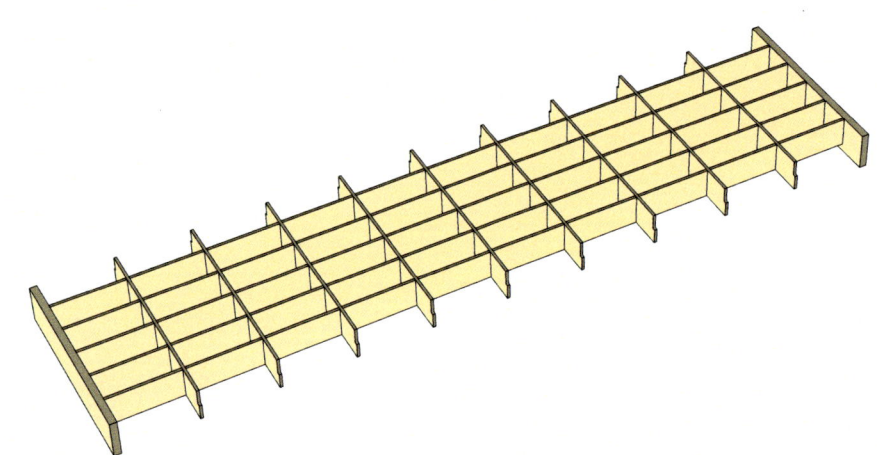

PRE-ASSEMBLING AND ADJUSTMENT

4

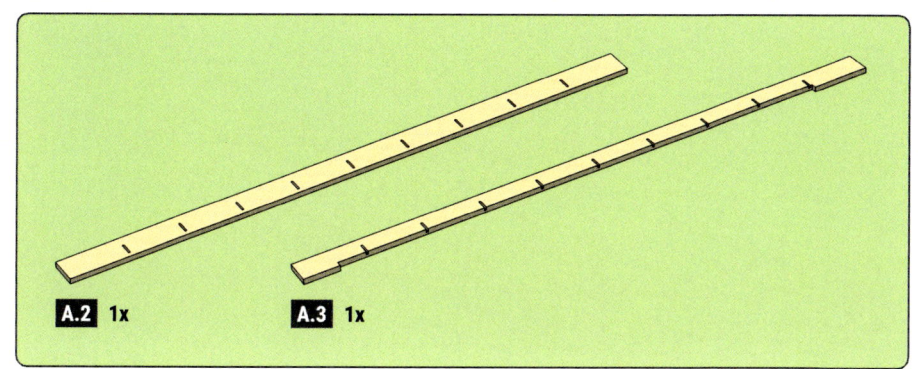

A.2 1x A.3 1x

4.1

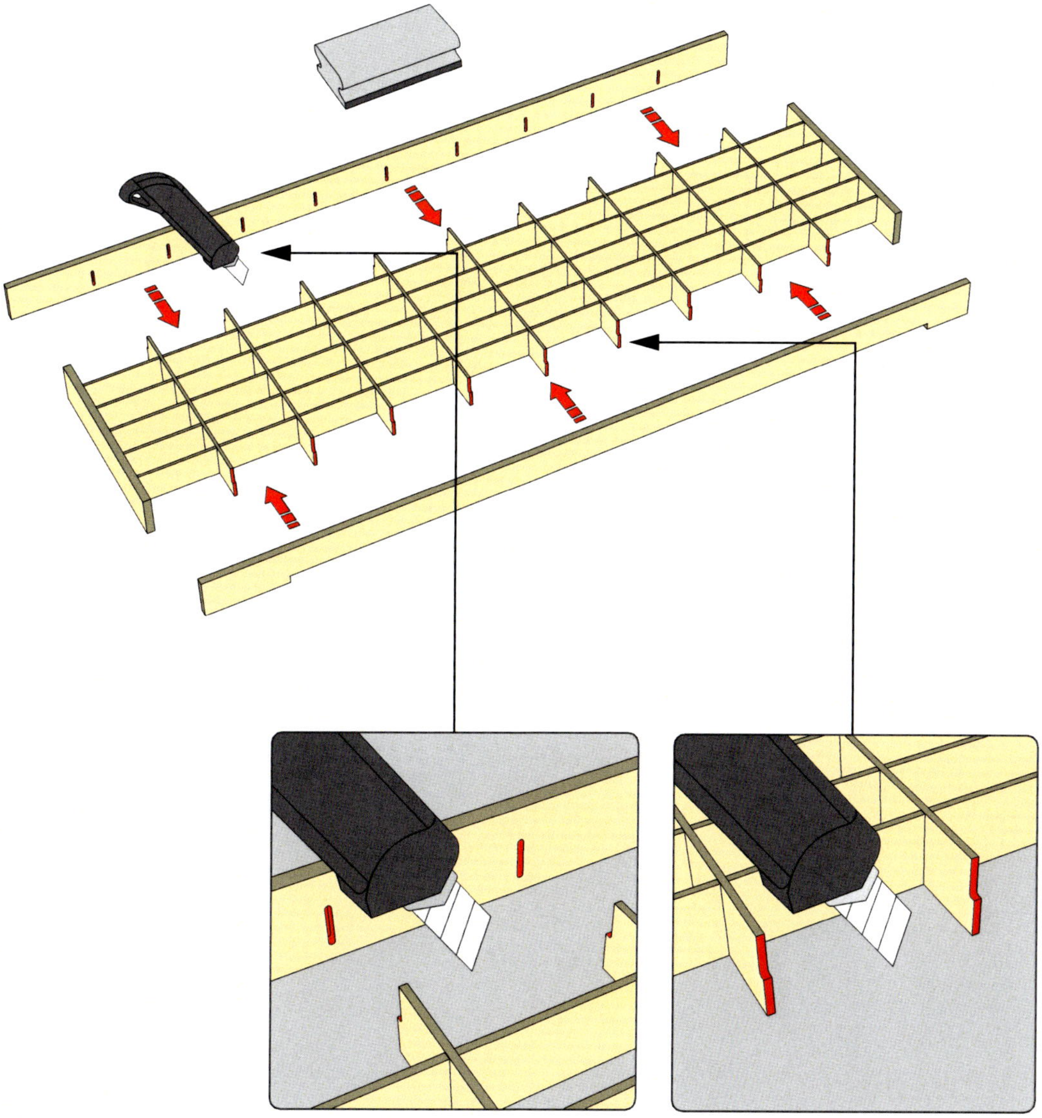

PRE-ASSEMBLING AND ADJUSTMENT

4.2

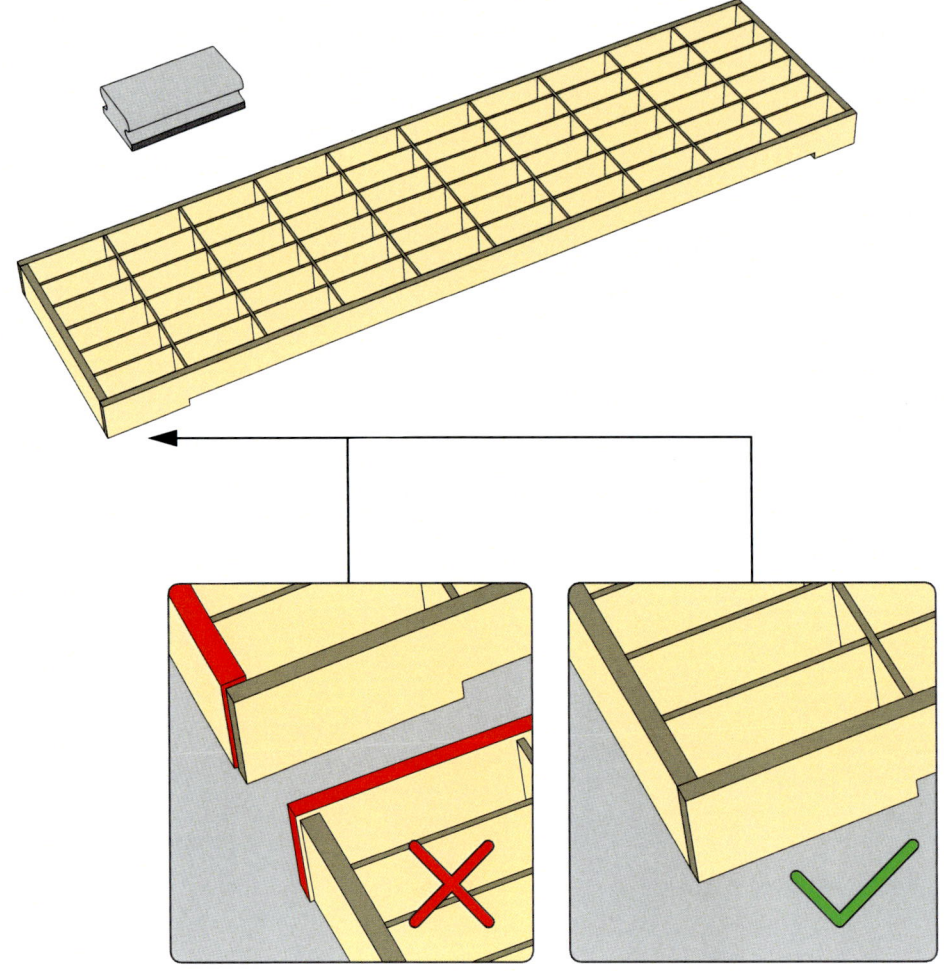

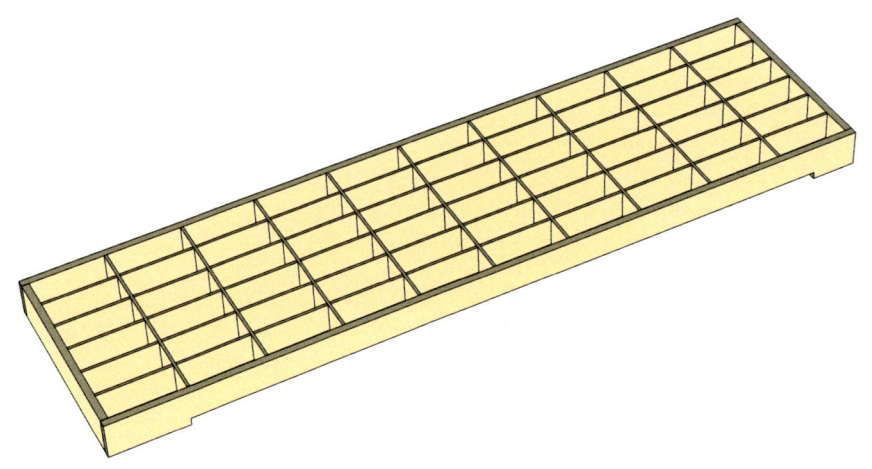

PRE-ASSEMBLING AND ADJUSTMENT

5

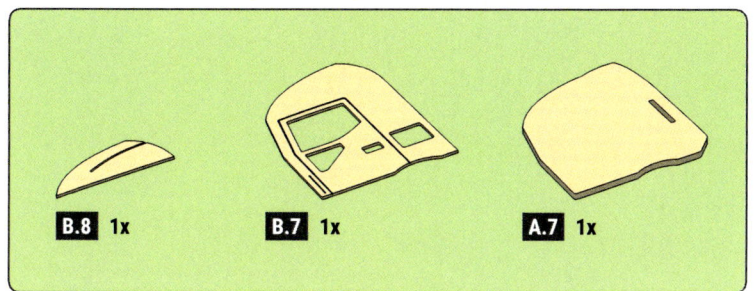

B.8 1x   **B.7** 1x   **A.7** 1x

5.1

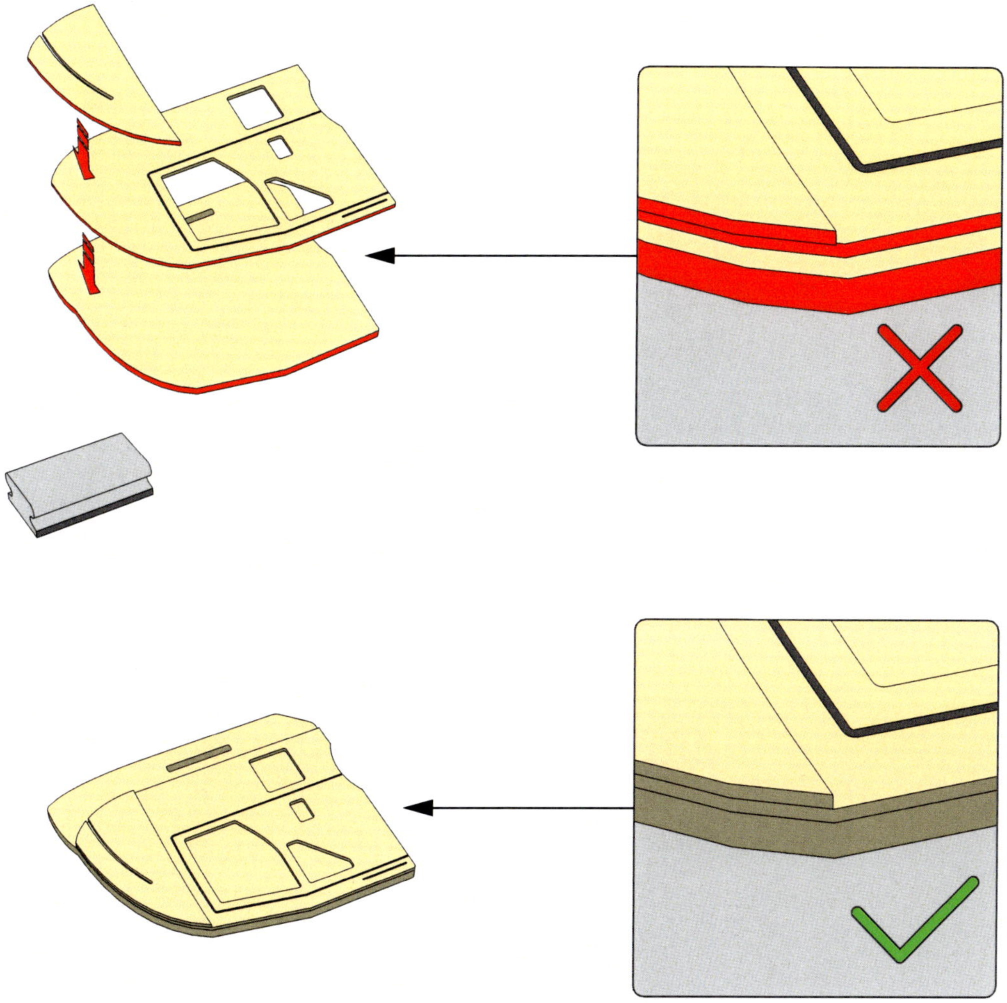

PRE-ASSEMBLING AND ADJUSTMENT

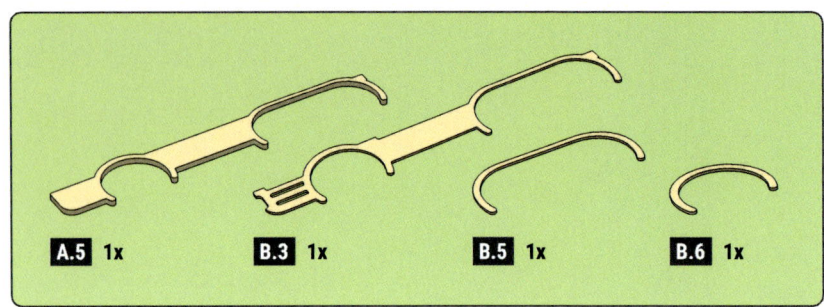

A.5 1x   B.3 1x   B.5 1x   B.6 1x

6.1

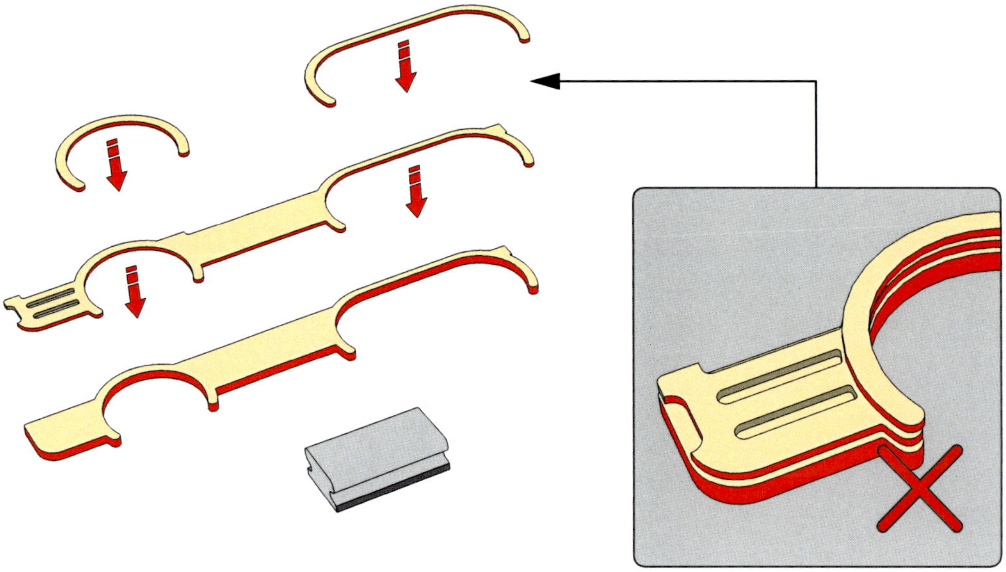

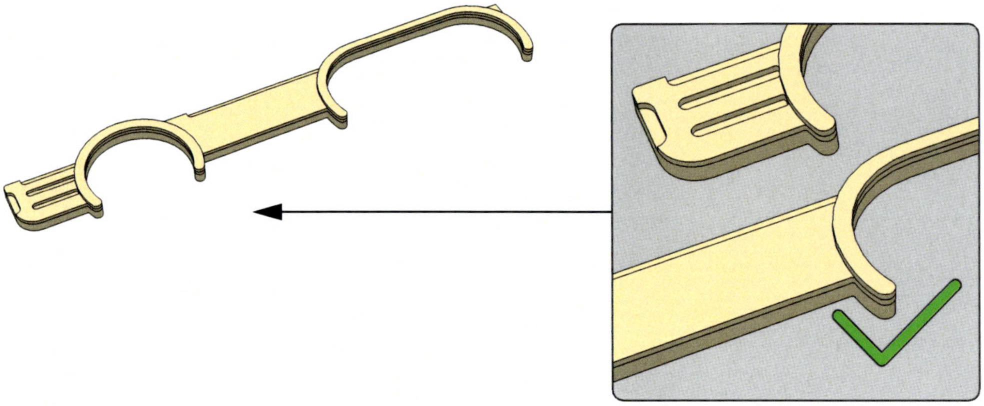

PRE-ASSEMBLING AND ADJUSTMENT

7

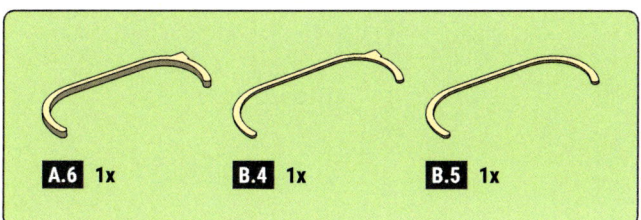

A.6 1x   **B.4** 1x   **B.5** 1x

7.1

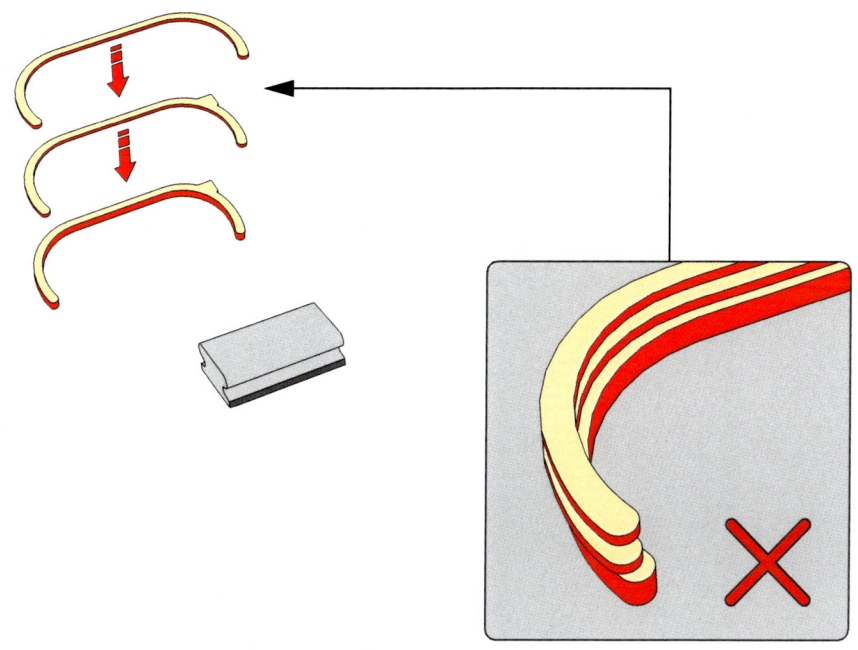
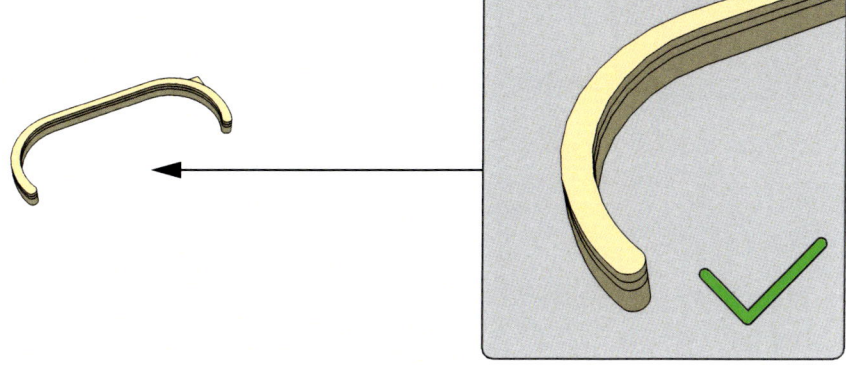

33

PRE-ASSEMBLING AND ADJUSTMENT

8

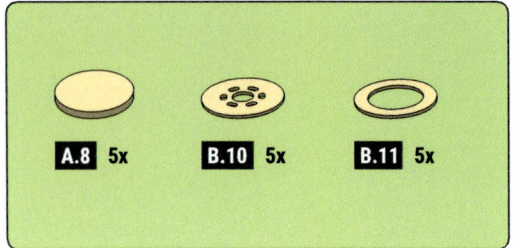

8.1

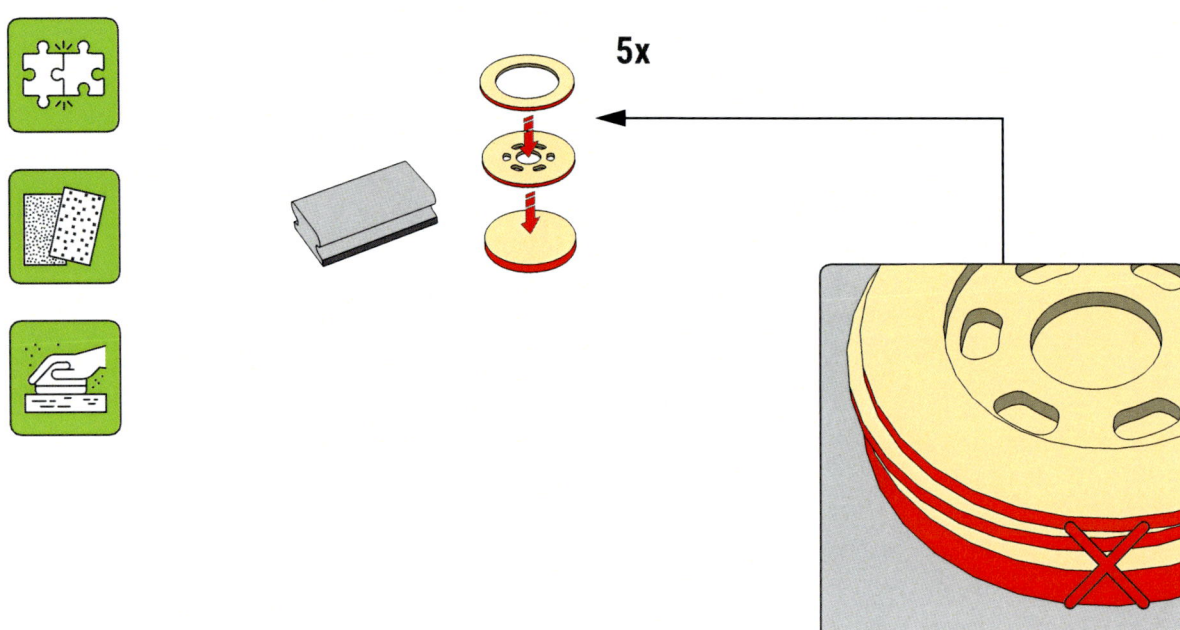

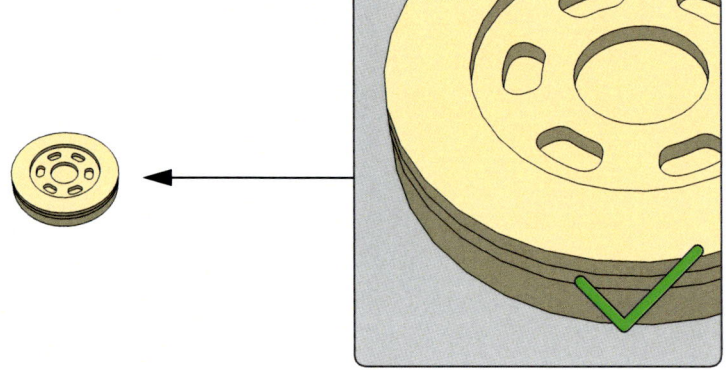

FINAL ASSEMBLING

FINAL ASSEMBLING

IMPORTANT NOTICE

- **The amount of time indicated on the "waiting time" icon is approximate. The exact timing depends on what kind of glue you use. Please read the information on the pack of your adhesive.**

Now that all the parts have been carefully fitted, you can start final assembling using glue.

In addition to protective equipment and glue, in this part you will also need a rubber mallet and different types of clamps.

We recommend using PVA wood glue as adhesive.

Be careful when installing clamps to avoid displacement of the parts when gluing.

FINAL ASSEMBLING

9

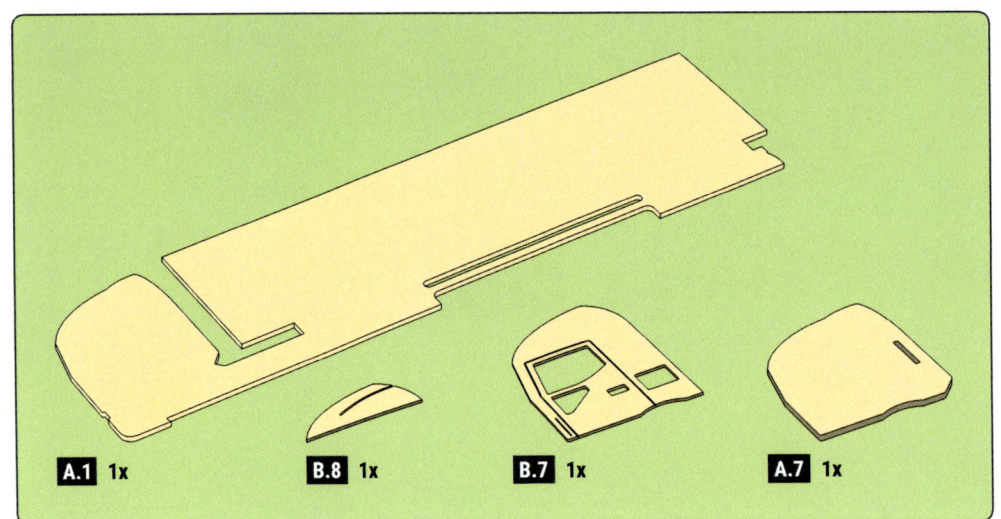

A.1 1x   B.8 1x   B.7 1x   A.7 1x

9.1

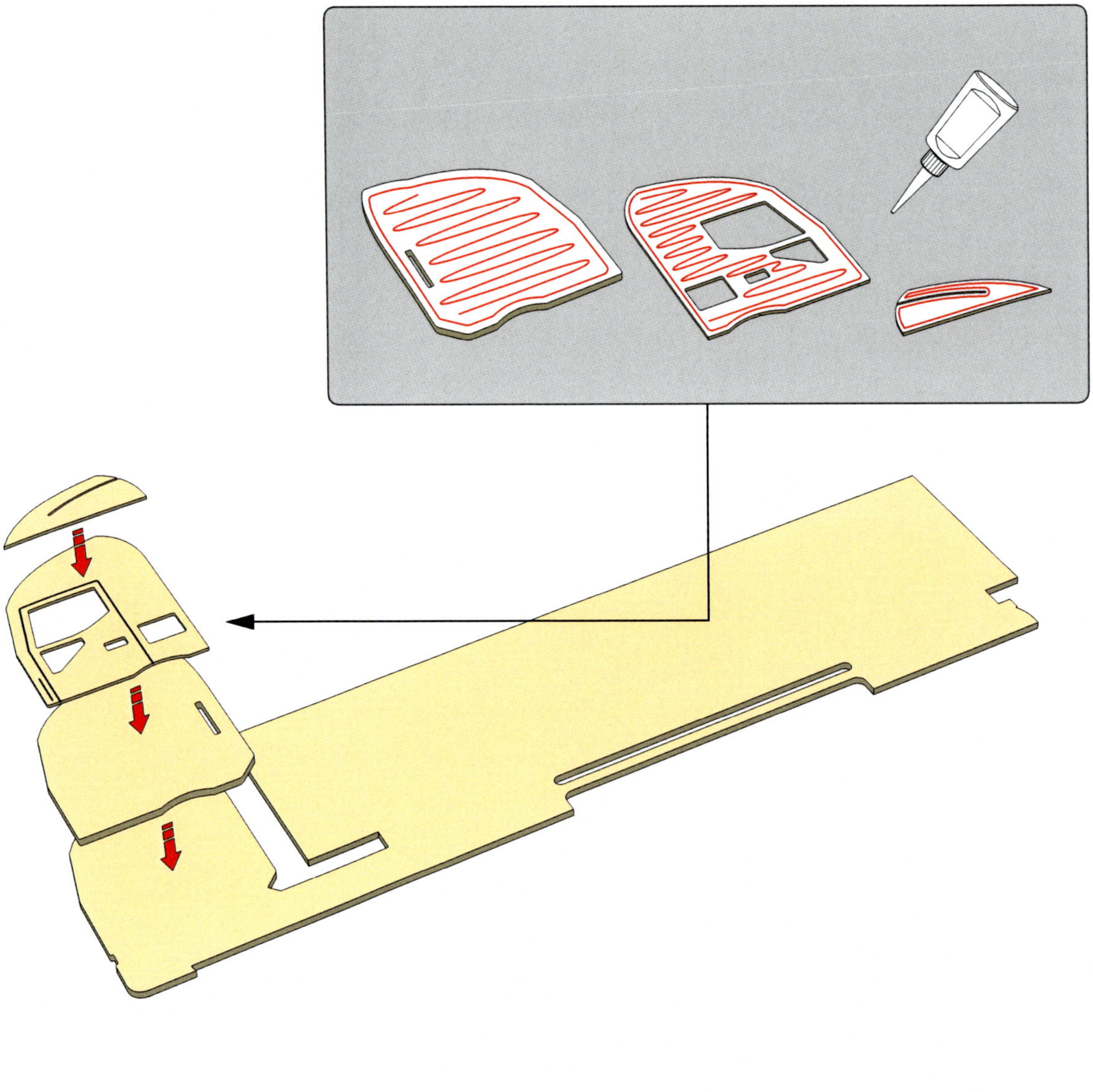

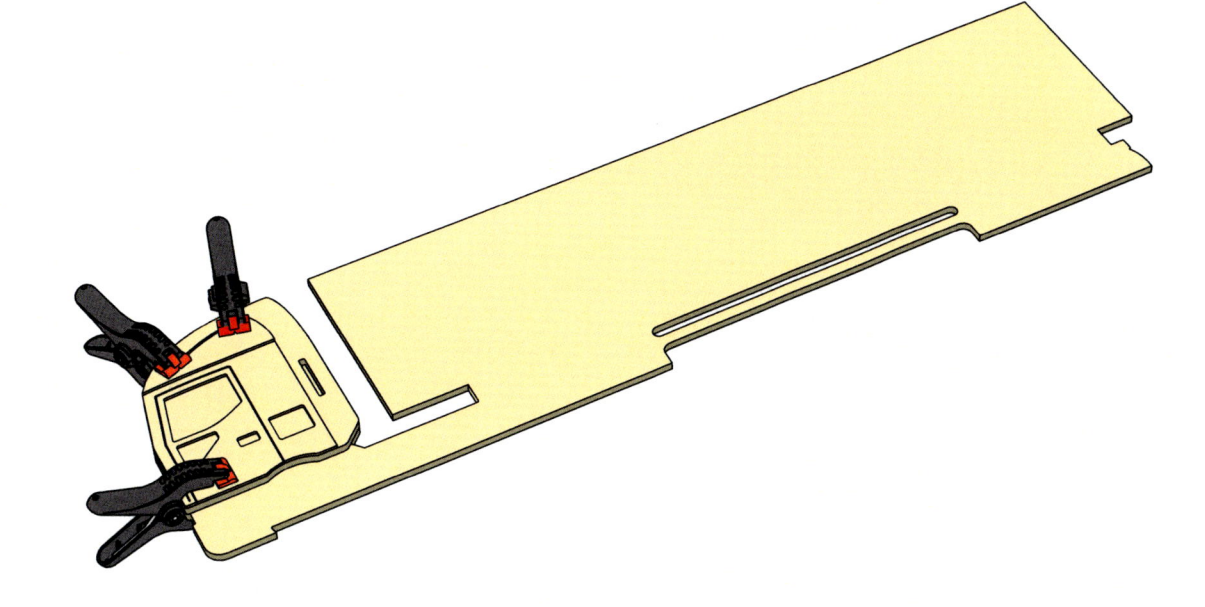

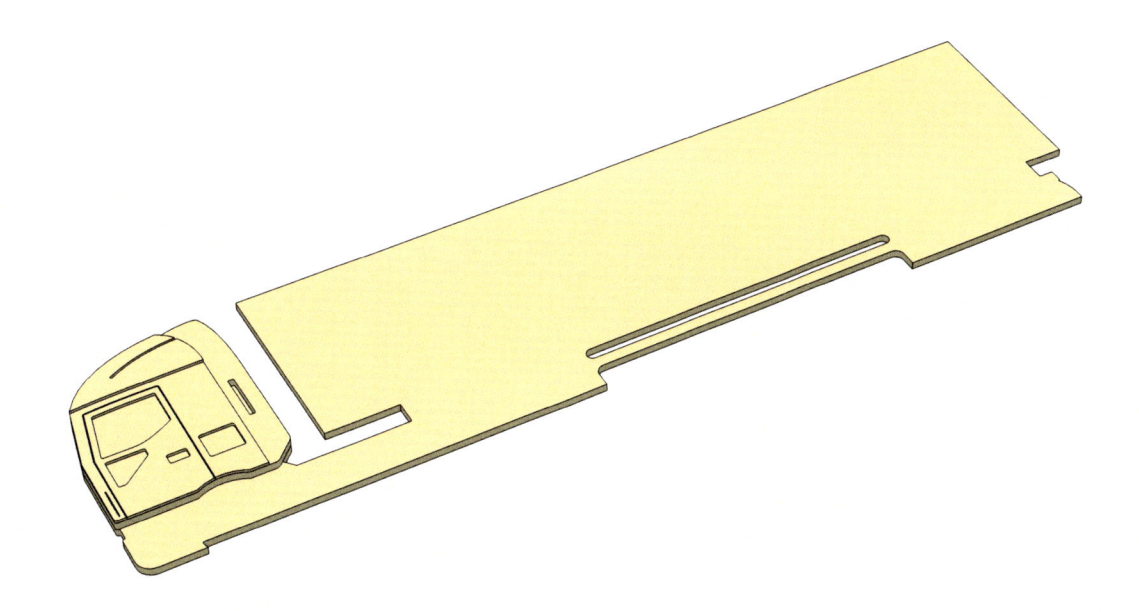

FINAL ASSEMBLING

9.2

9.3

FINAL ASSEMBLING

10

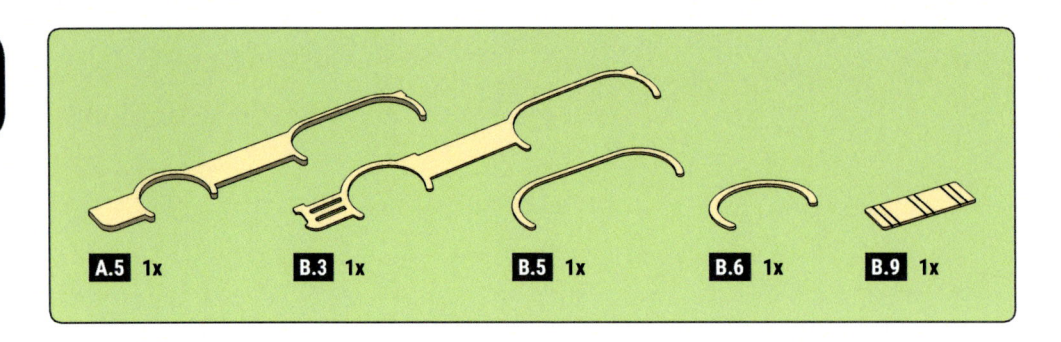

A.5 1x **B.3** 1x **B.5** 1x **B.6** 1x **B.9** 1x

10.1

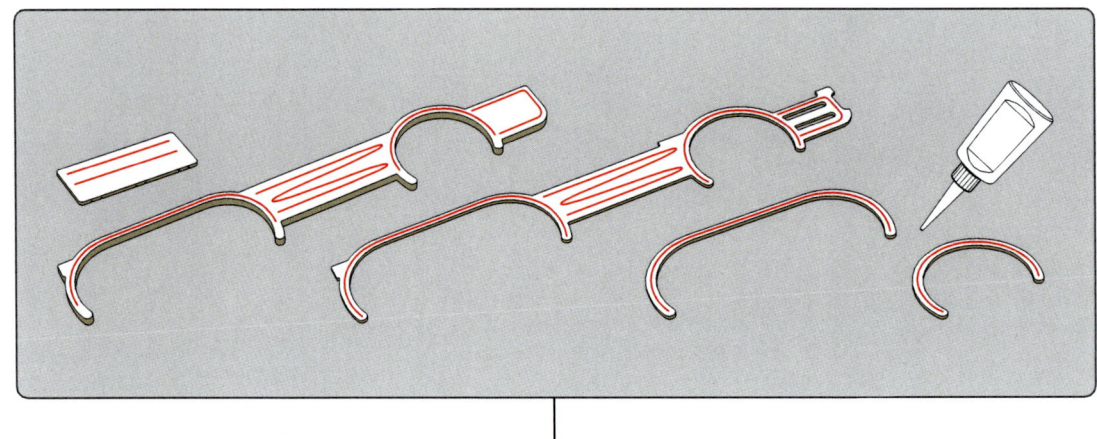

GLUE
FLIP

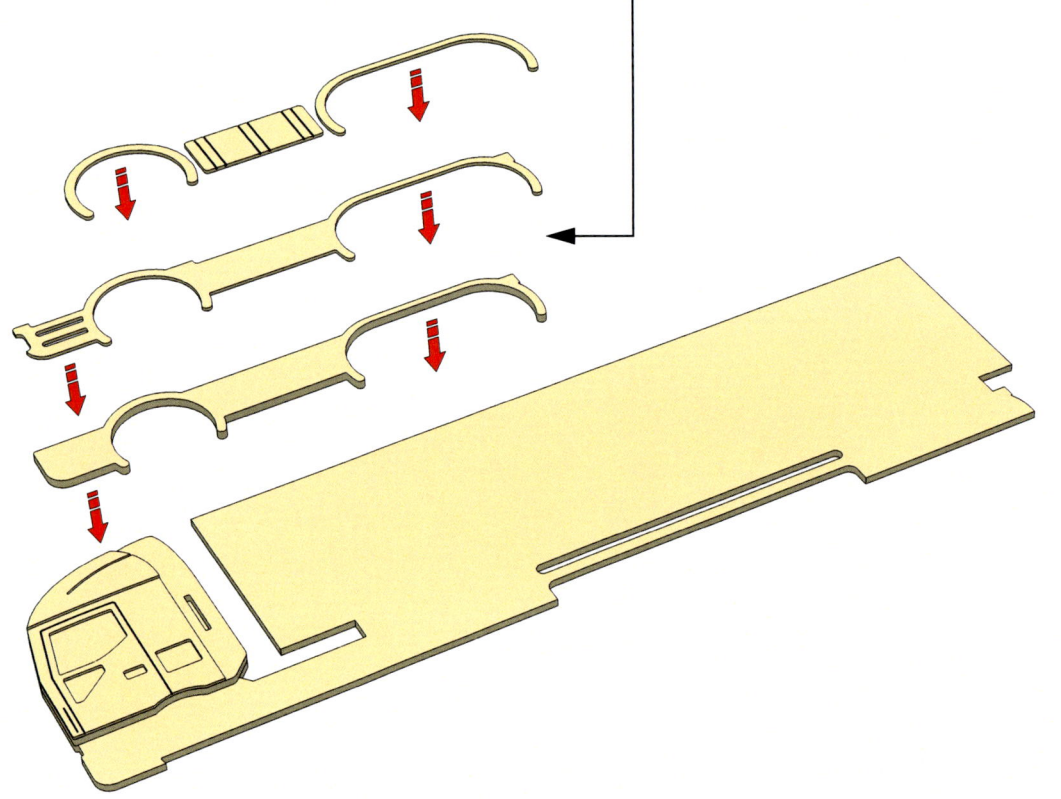

38

FINAL ASSEMBLING

10.2

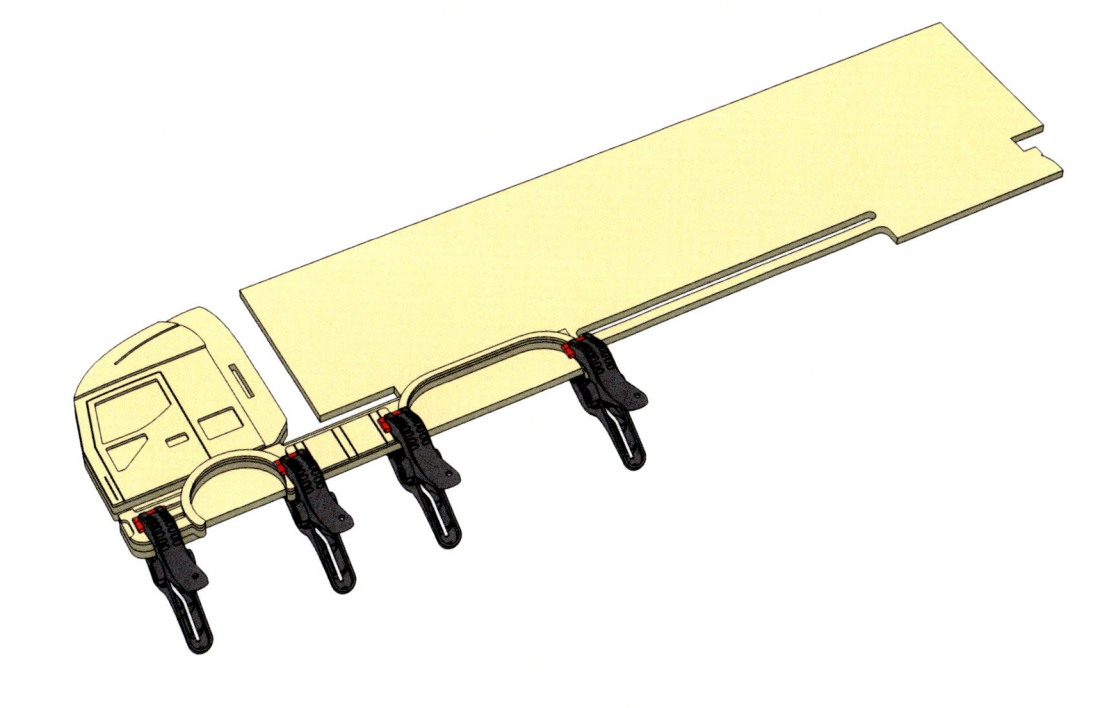

10.3

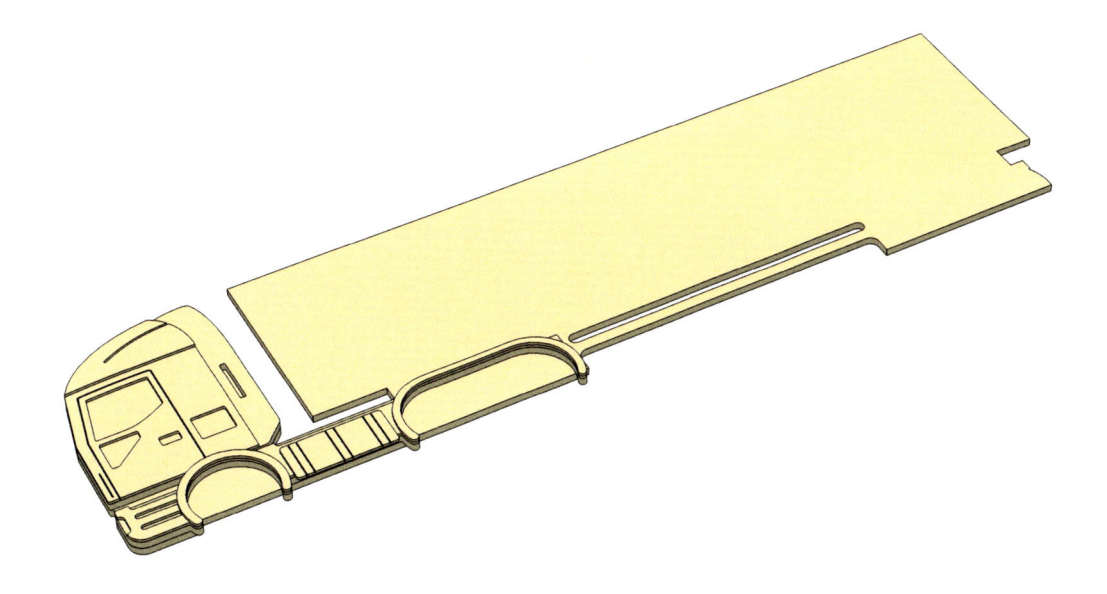

FINAL ASSEMBLING

11

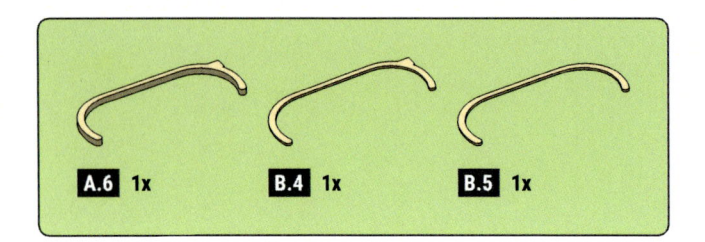

A.6 1x   **B.4** 1x   **B.5** 1x

11.1

40

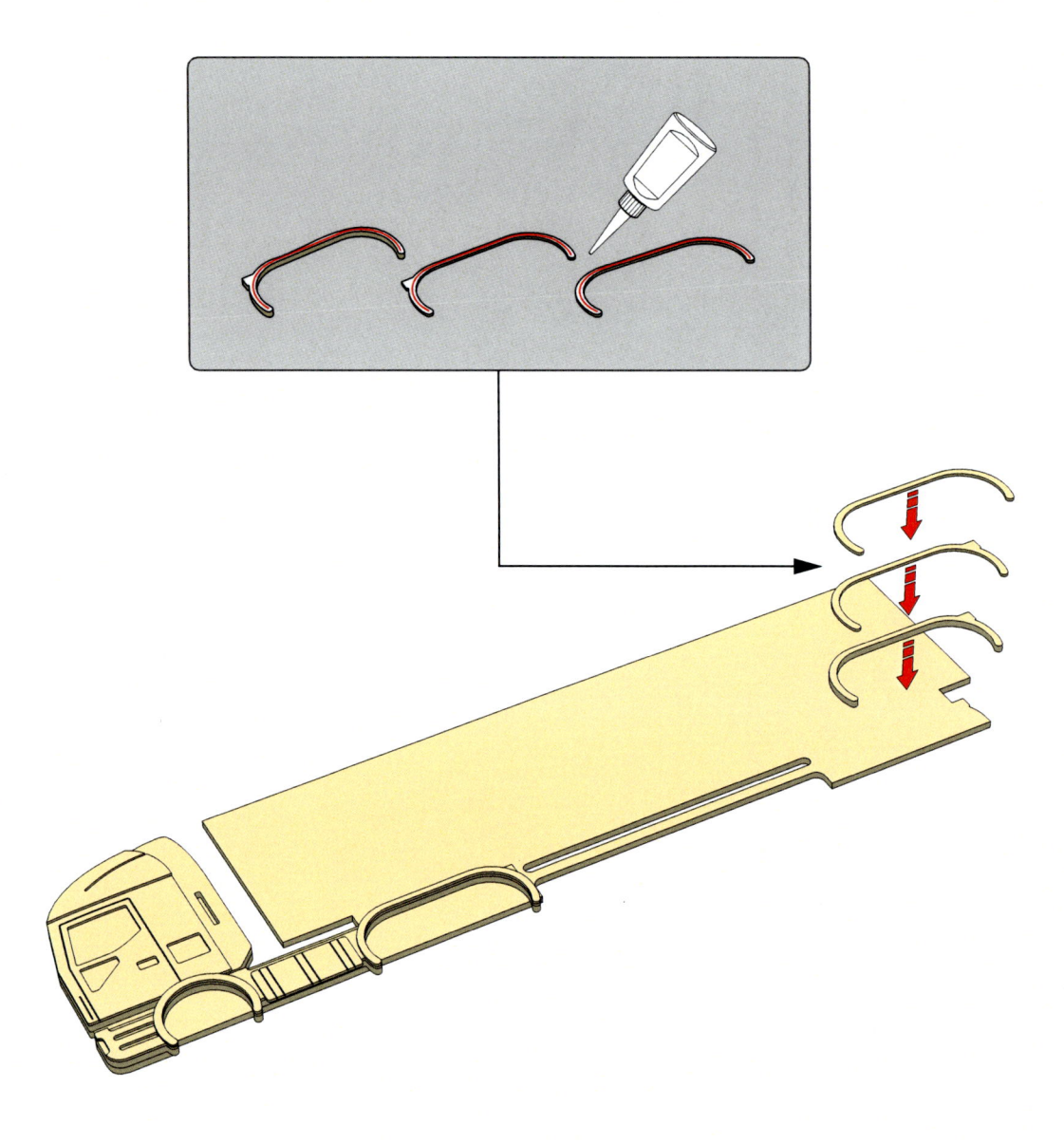

FINAL ASSEMBLING

11.2

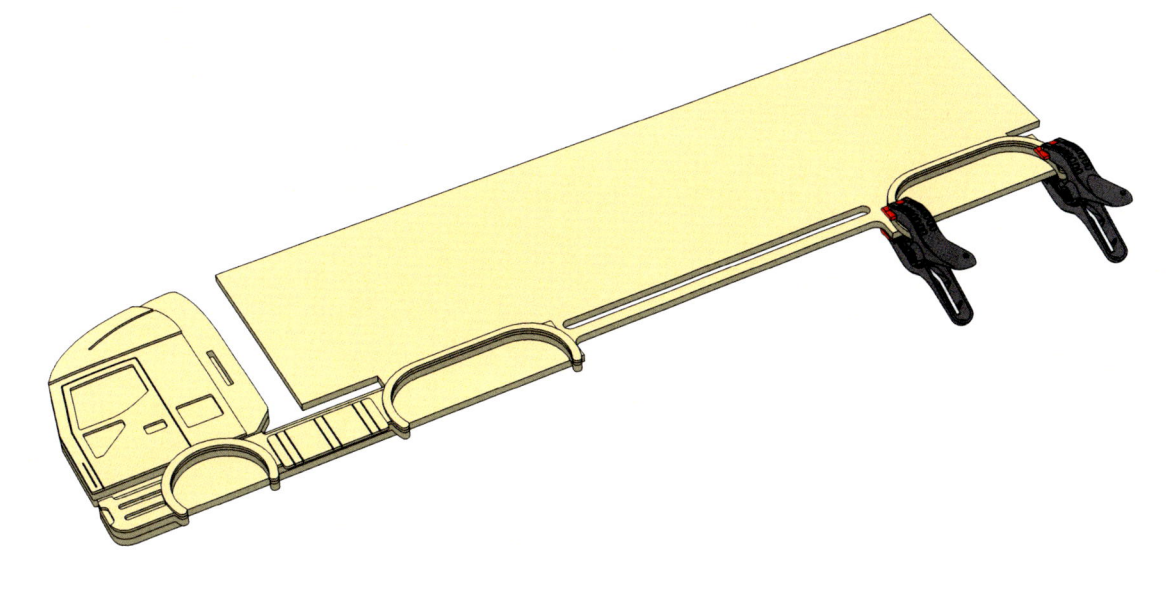

11.3

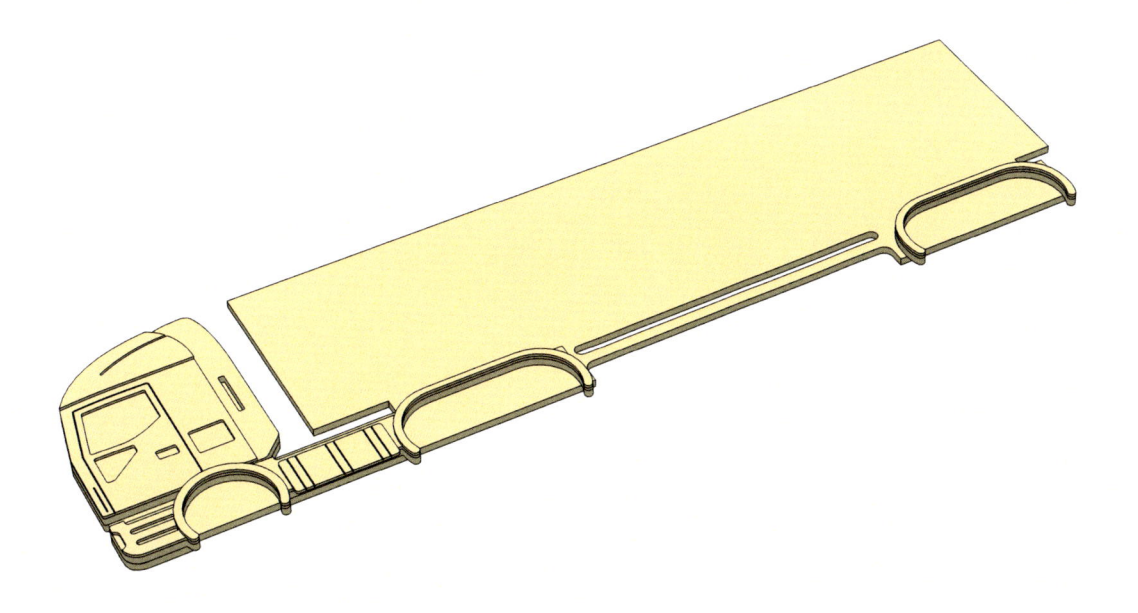

41

FINAL ASSEMBLING

12

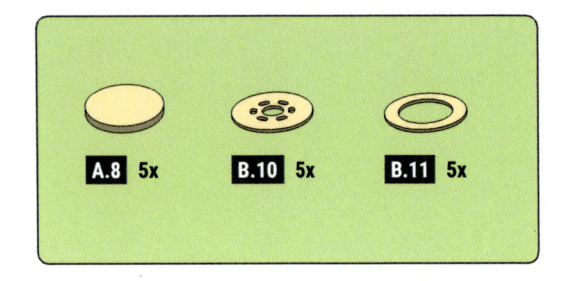

| A.8 5x | B.10 5x | B.11 5x |

12.1

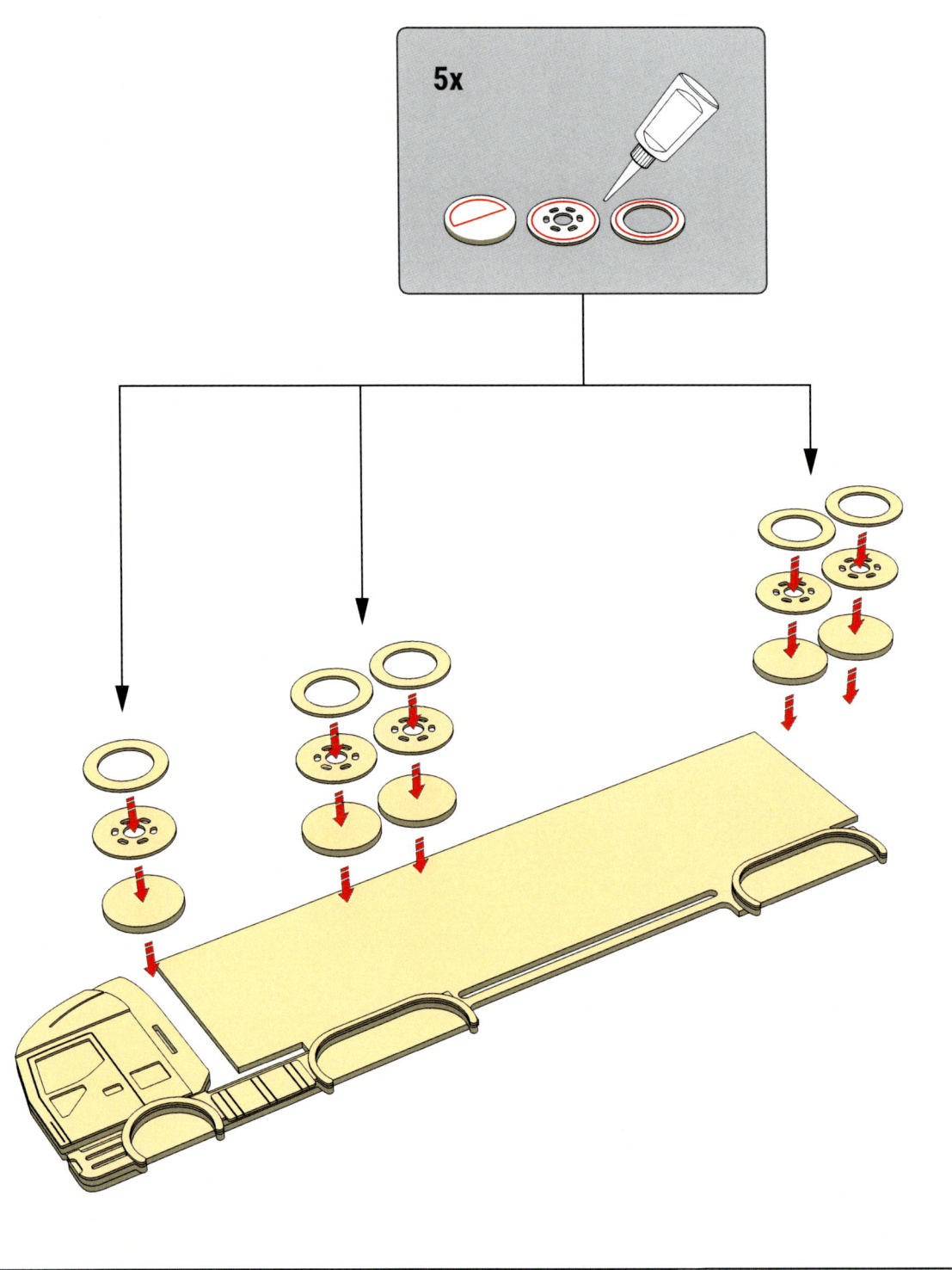

GLUE

FLIP

5x

42

FINAL ASSEMBLING

12.2

15min

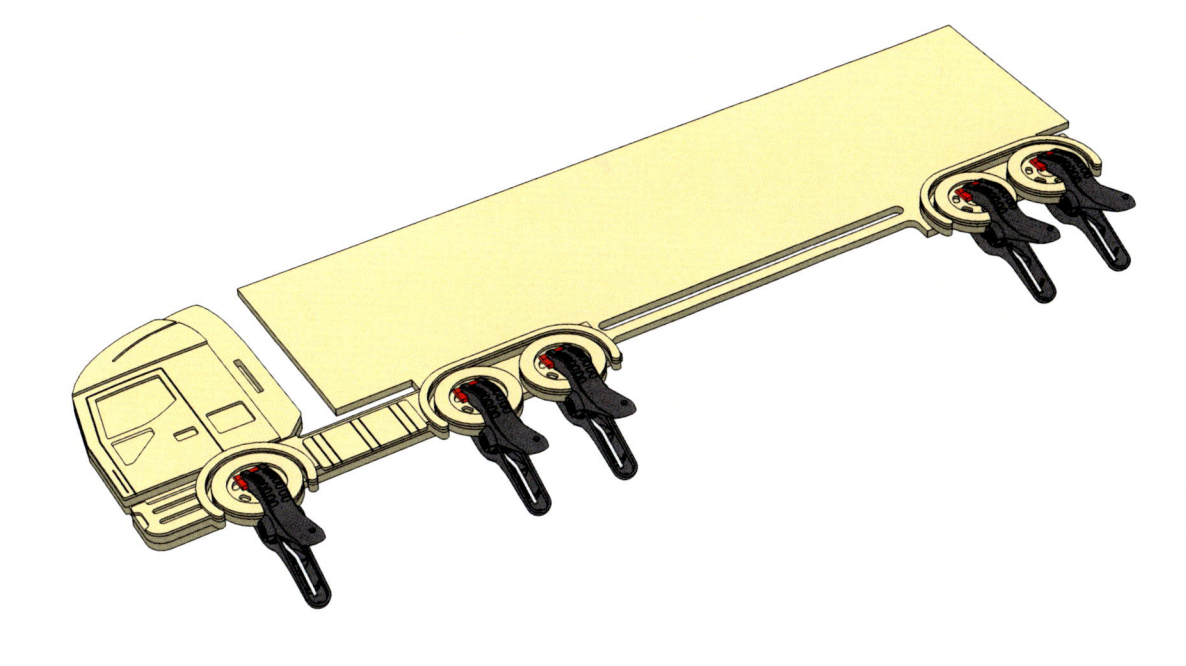

12.3

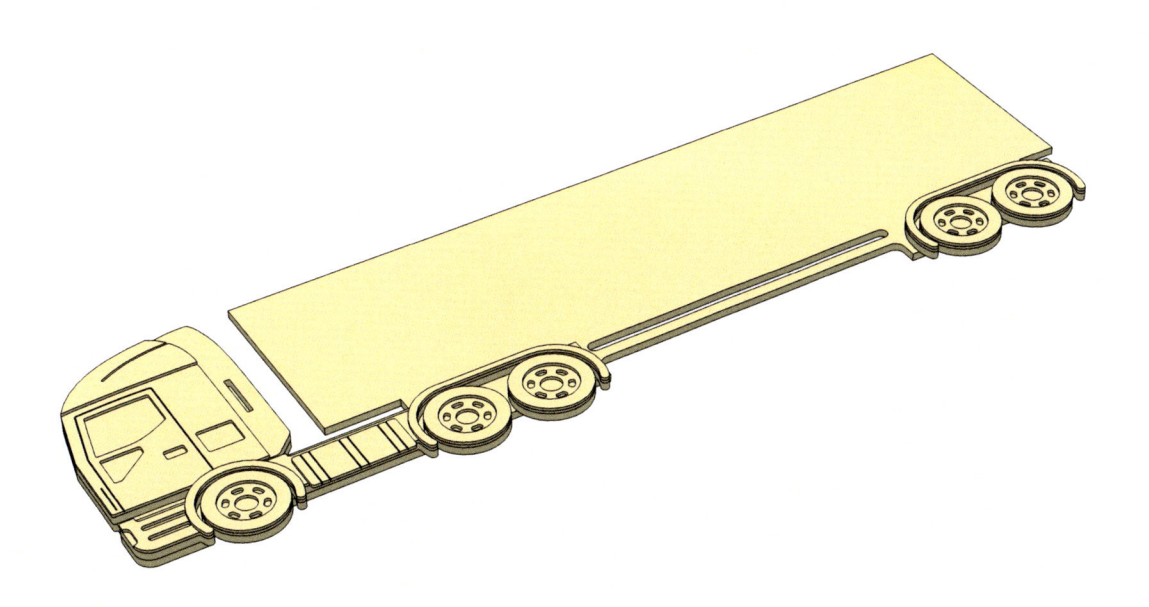

43

FINAL ASSEMBLING

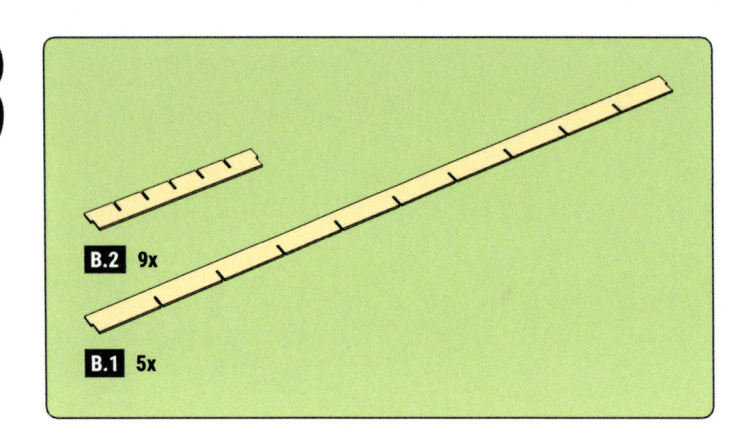

13

B.2 9x
B.1 5x

13.1

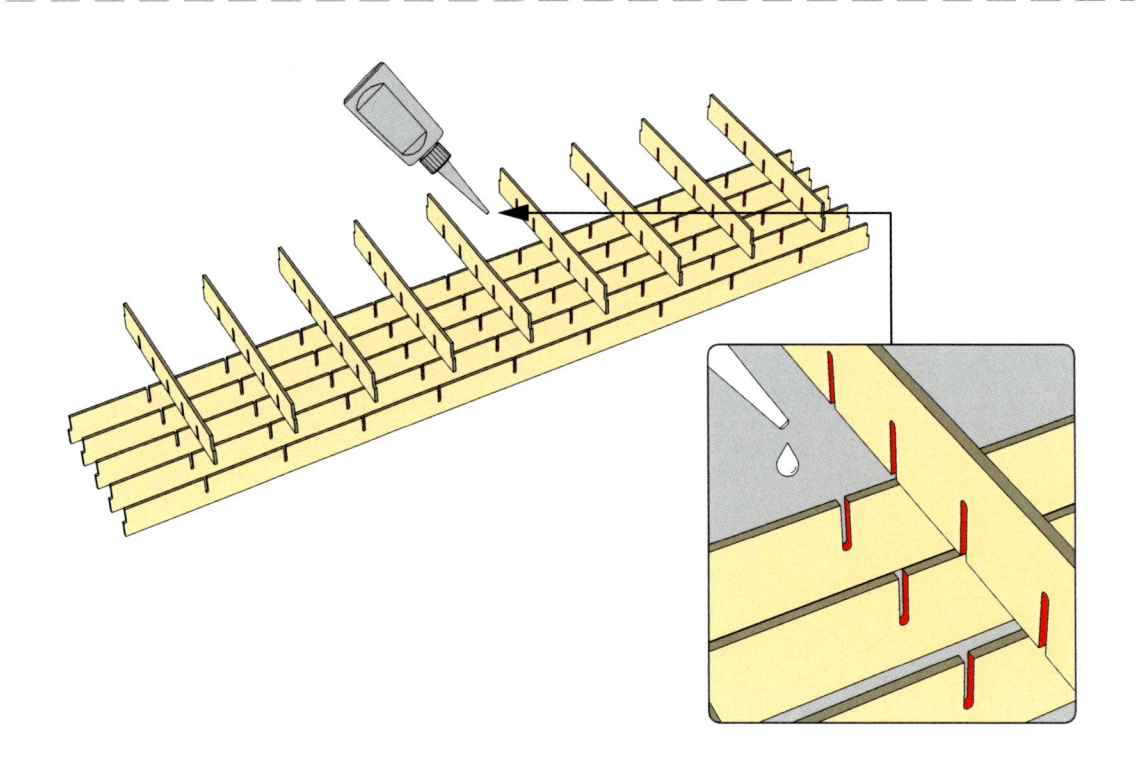

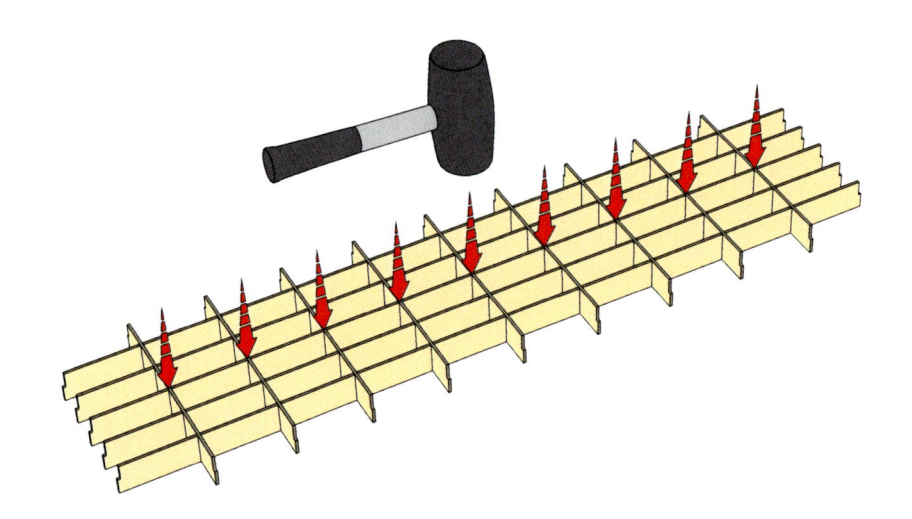

13.2

44

FINAL ASSEMBLING

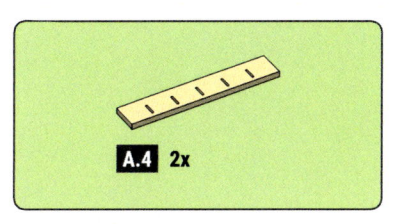

14

A.4 2x

14.1

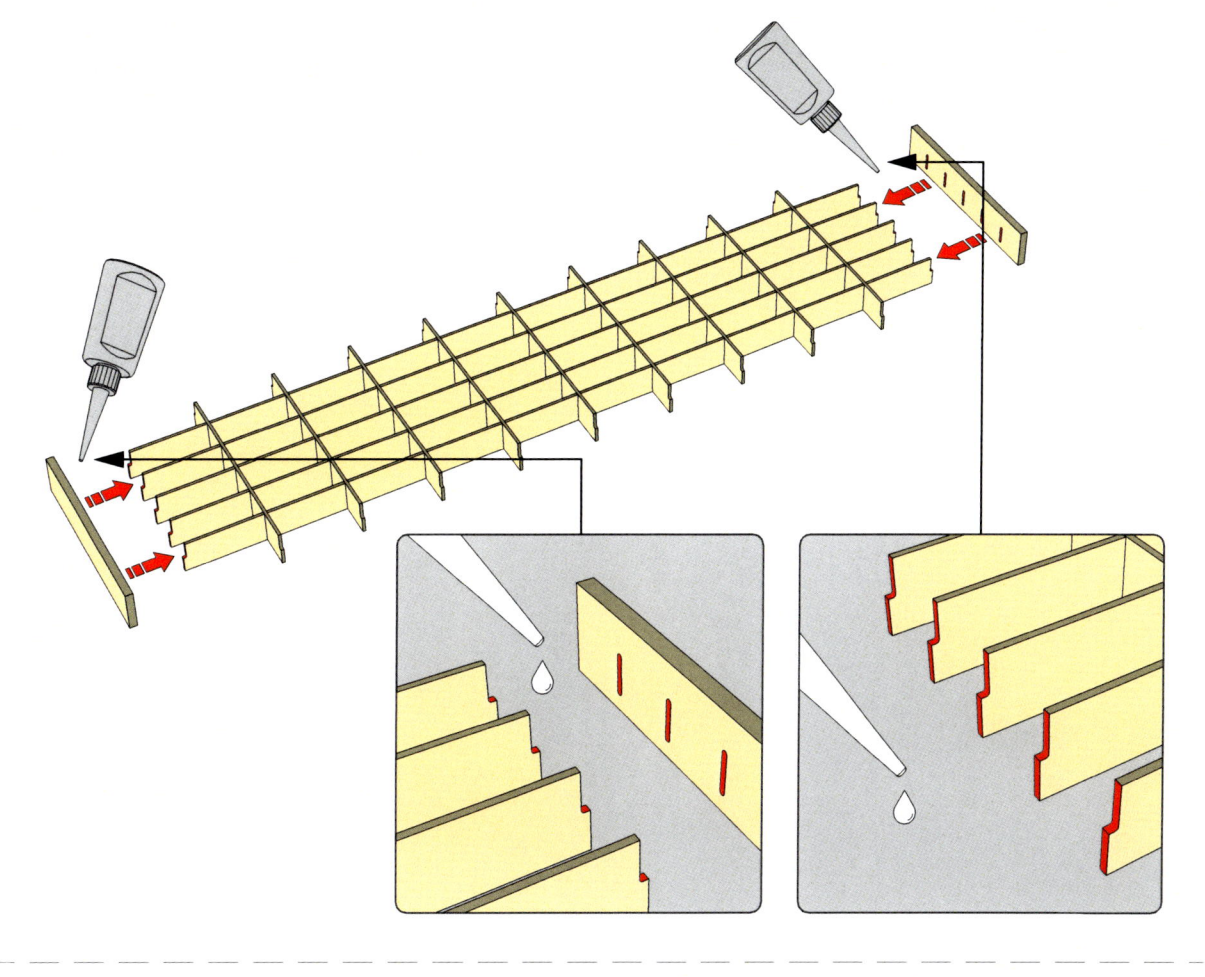

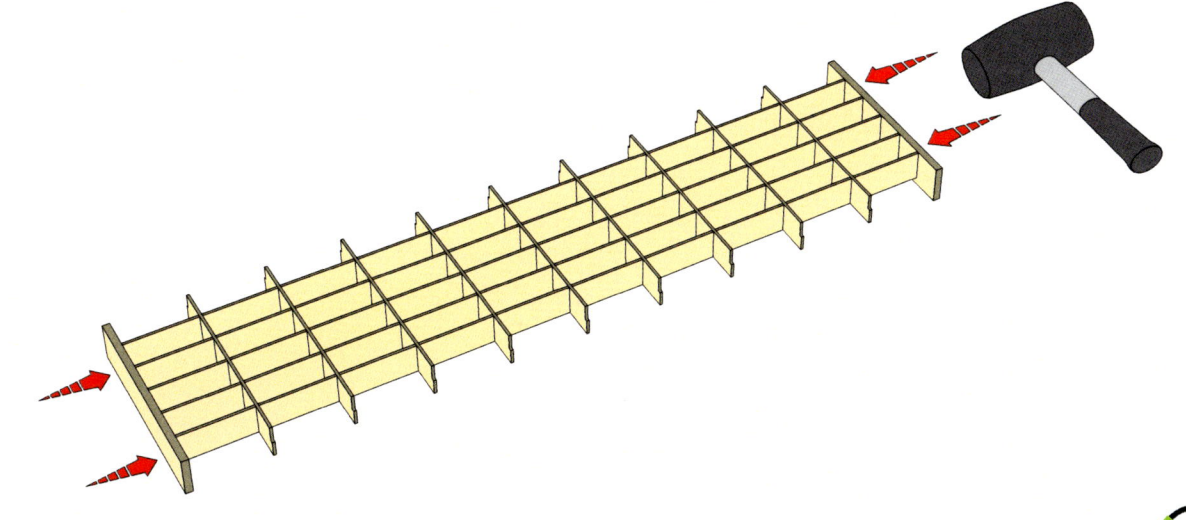

14.2

FINAL ASSEMBLING

15

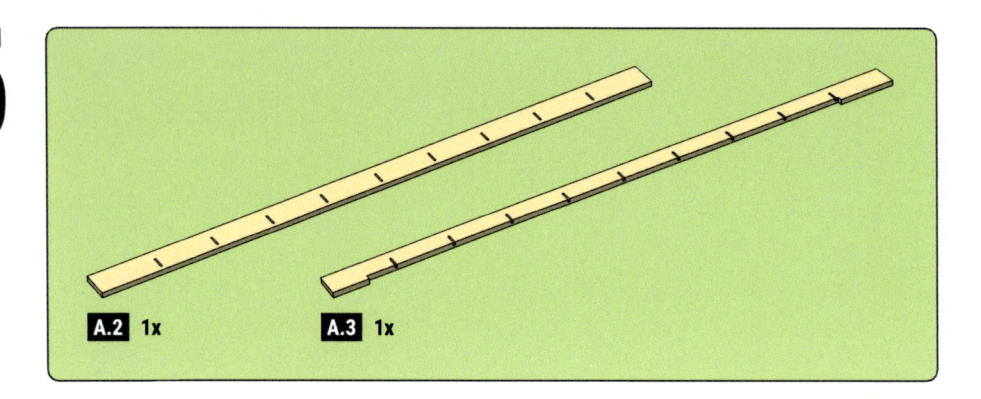

A.2 1x **A.3** 1x

15.1

46

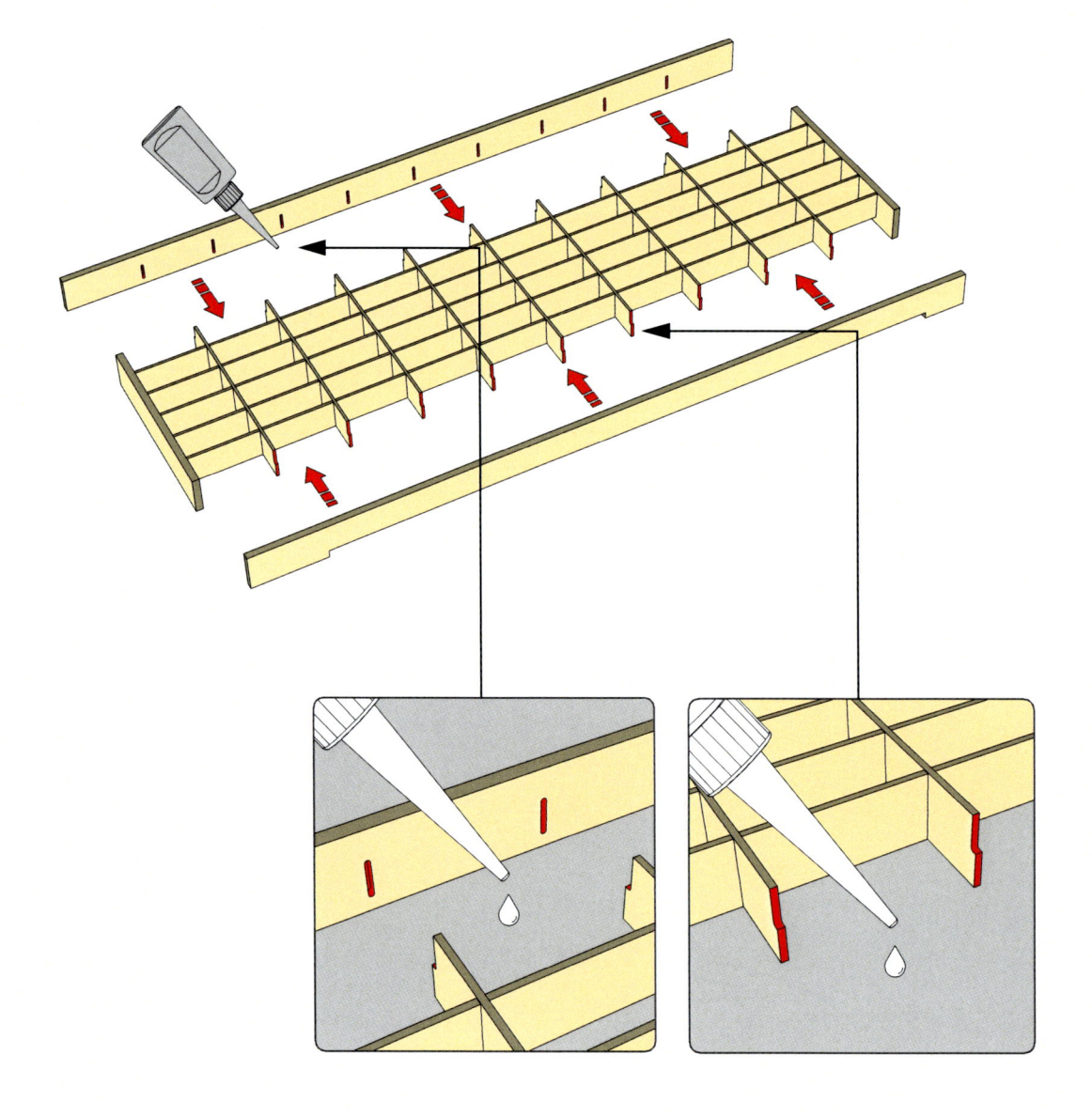

FINAL ASSEMBLING

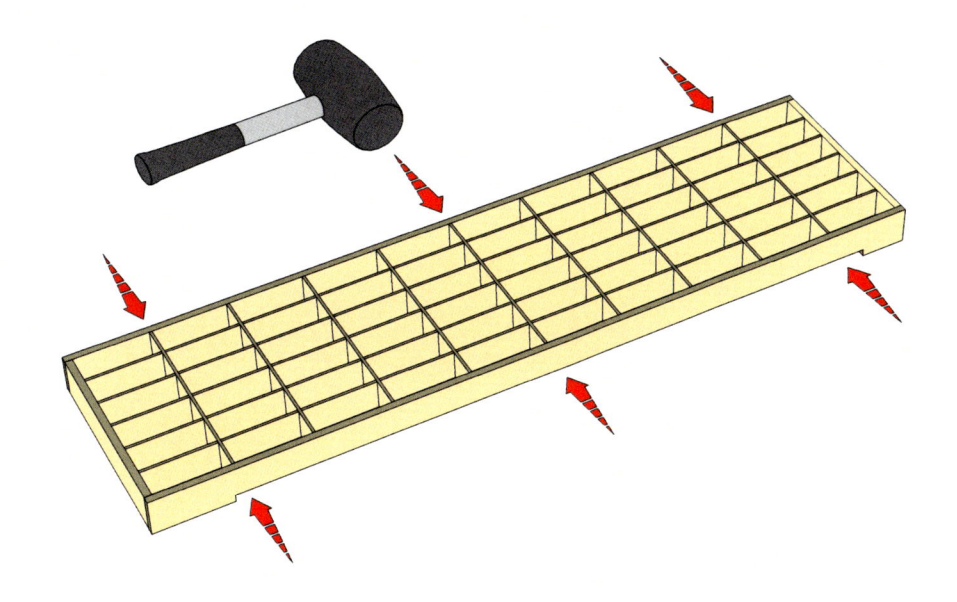

15.2

15.3

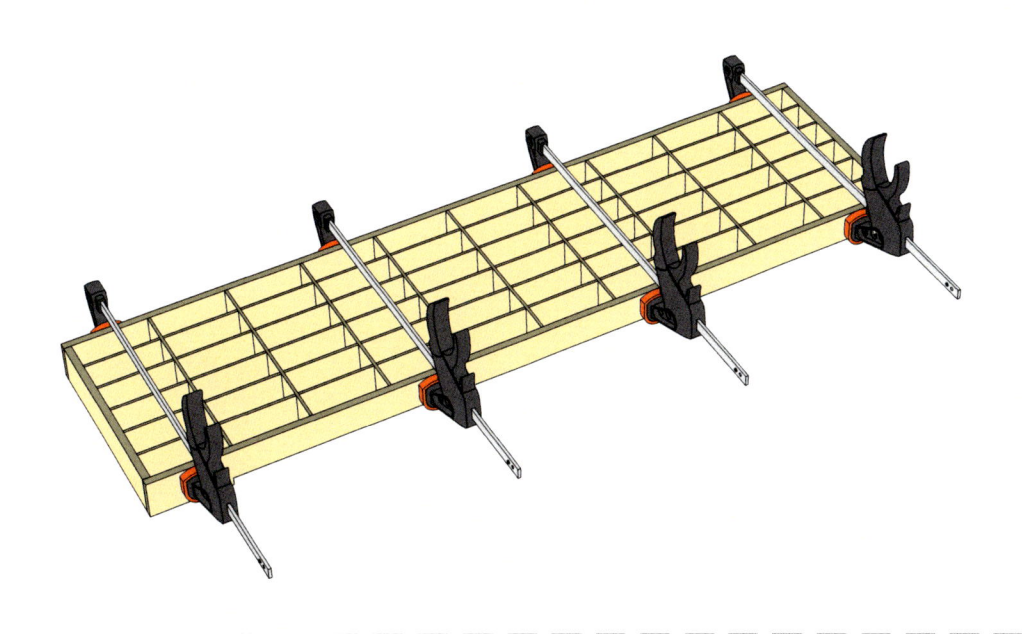

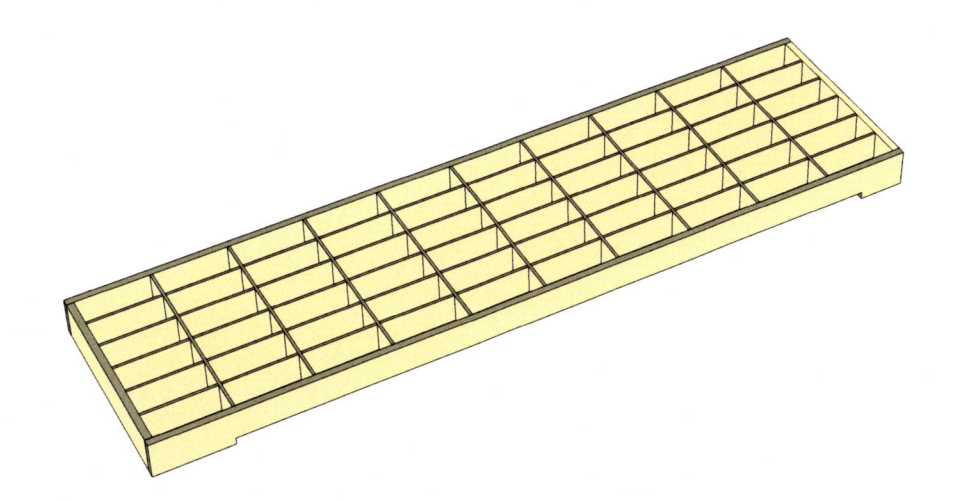

15 min

15.4

47

FINAL ASSEMBLING

16

12.3 Page 42

15.4 Page 46

16.1

GLUE

FLIP

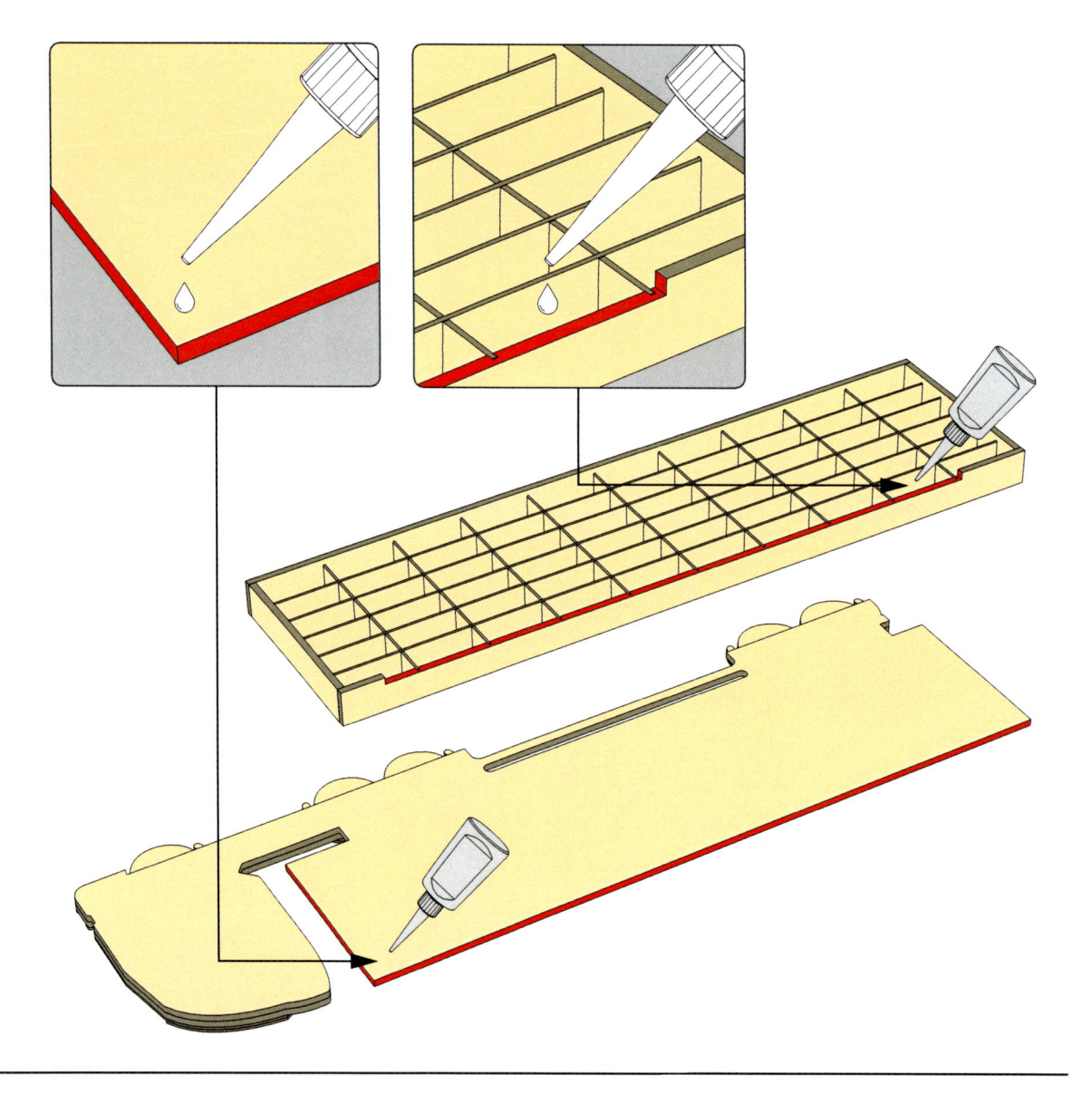

48

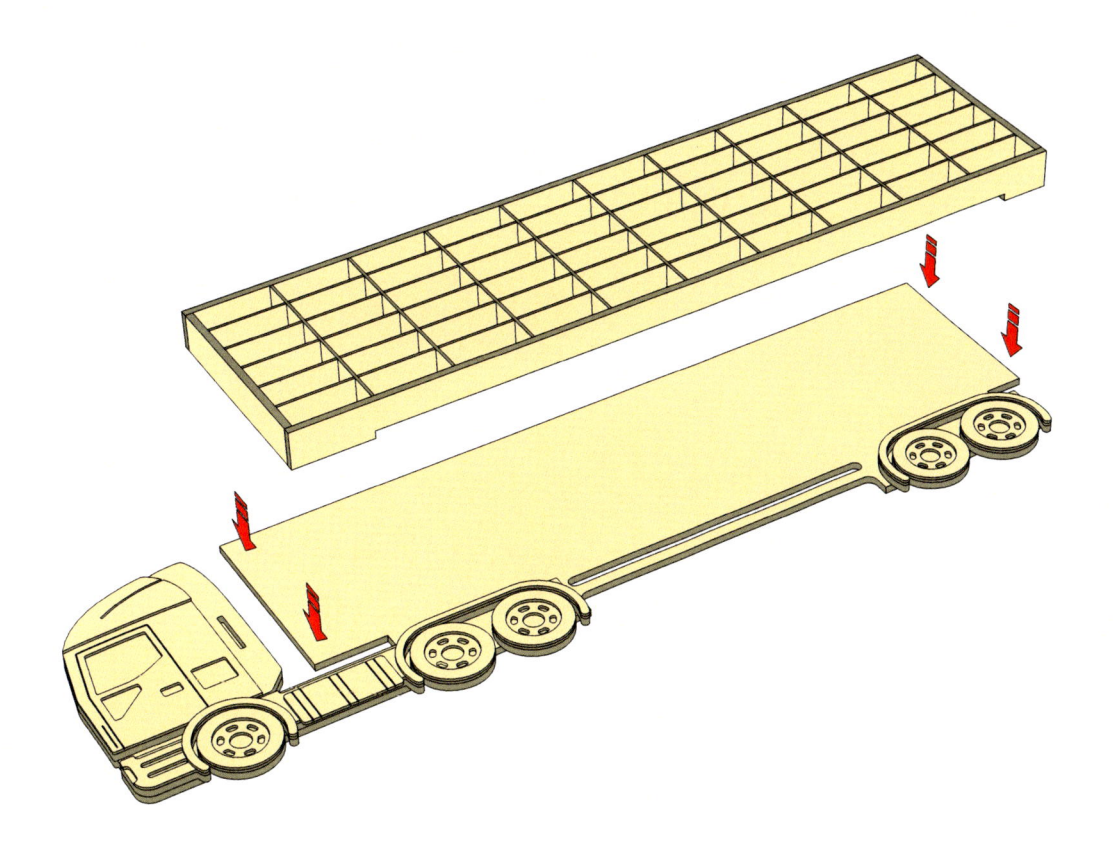

FINAL ASSEMBLING

16.2

49

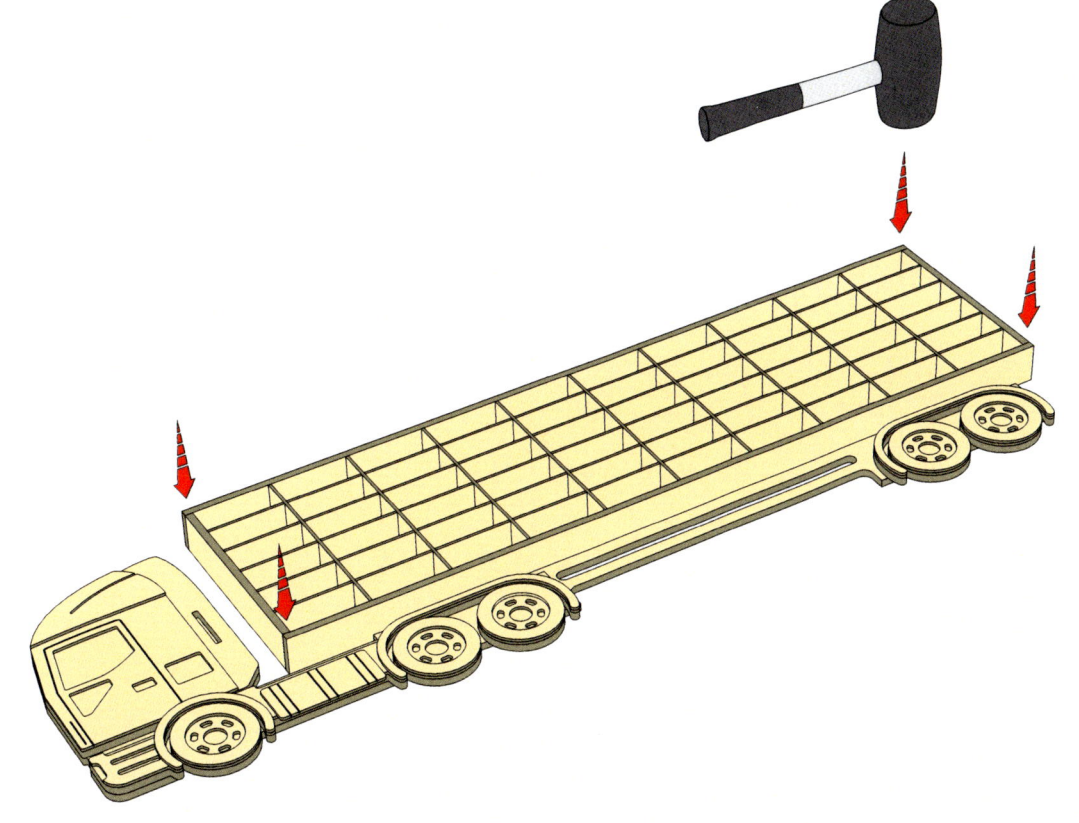

FINAL ASSEMBLING

16.3

PAINTING AND DRYING

IMPORTANT NOTICE

- **The amount of time indicated on the "waiting time" icon is approximate. The exact timing depends on what kind of paint or varnish you use. Please read the information on the pack of your painting materials.**

- **We recommend to choose non-toxic, low-VOC painting materials and work in a well-ventilated area.**

At this final part of the project you will need fine-grit sandpaper, painting materials and a brush in addition to protective equipment. Be very careful and do not rush, because it is very easy to ruin the final result at this stage.

Make sure that assembled item is well cleaned from dust and protruding glue.

Apply a thin, even coat of primer to the assembled item and allow it to dry according to the manufacturer's instructions. After the primer is dry, you should lightly sand the surface to remove any raised fibers.

Apply the first coat of paint or varnish evenly, following the wood grain. Allow it to dry completely, which typically takes a few hours. You can lightly sand the surface again to ensure a very smooth finish.

Based on the coverage, apply the second coat (or more) for a more vibrant finish.
Be patient and allow sufficient time for the paint or varnish to dry and cure completely. This can take up to several days depending on the materials.

PAINTING AND DRYING

17 — PAINT ASSEMBLED ITEM WITH PREPARED PAINTING MATERIALS

17.1

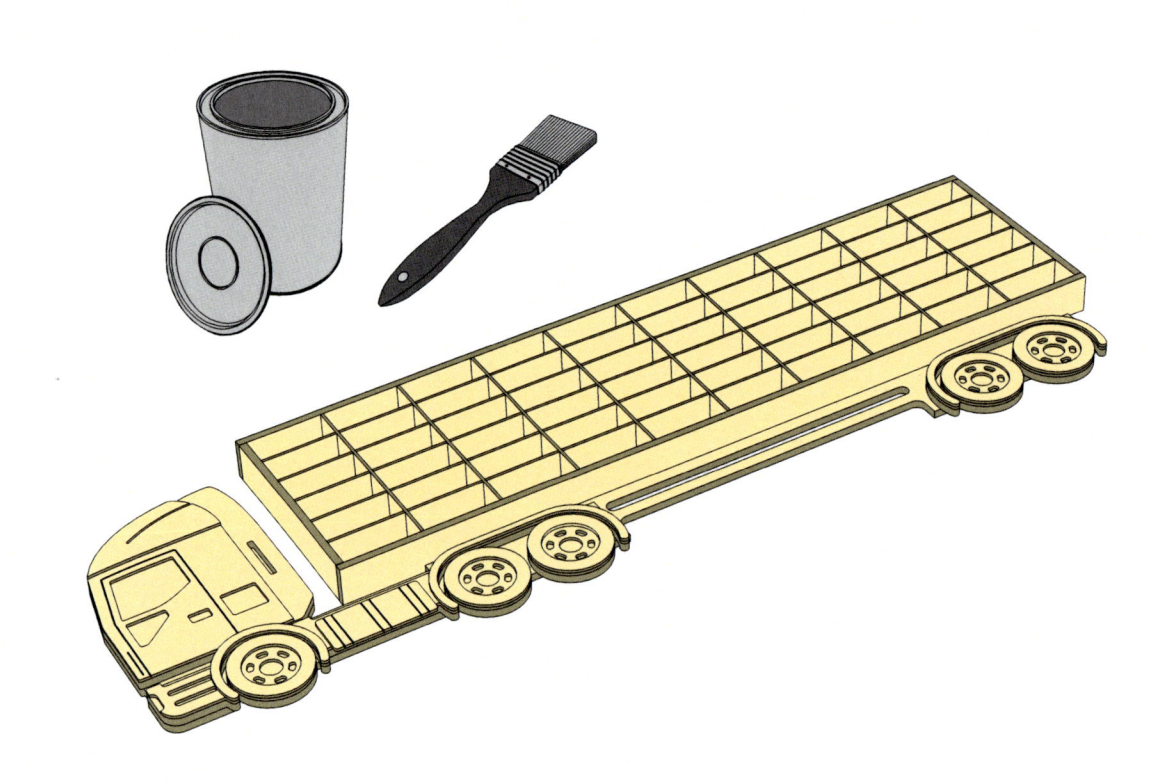

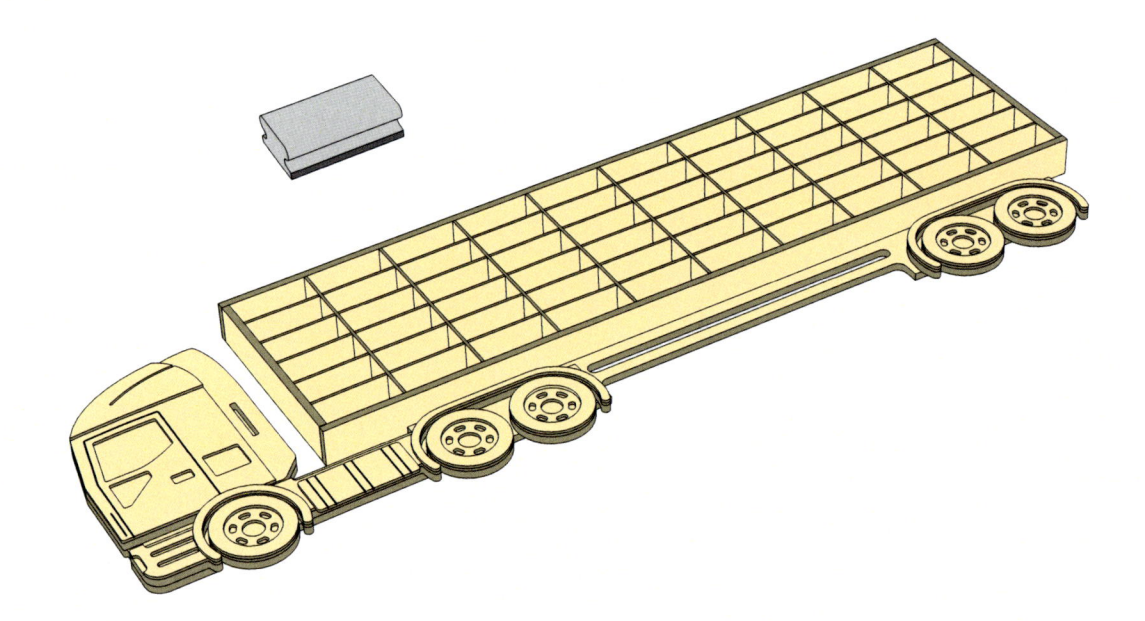

17.2

YOU MAY ALSO BE INTERESTED

Do not miss our new projects and updates

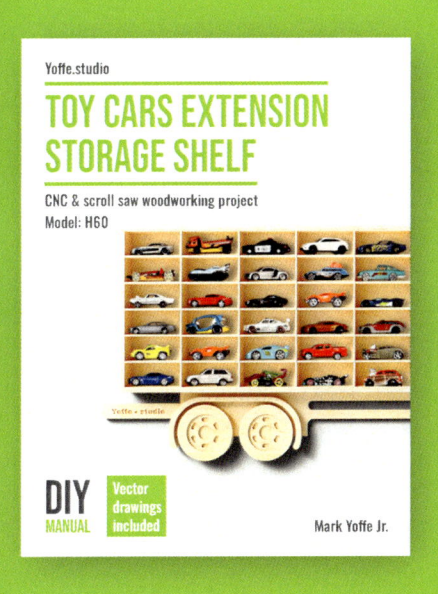

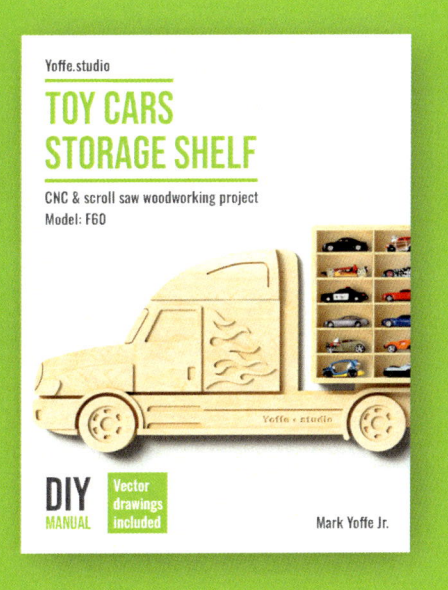

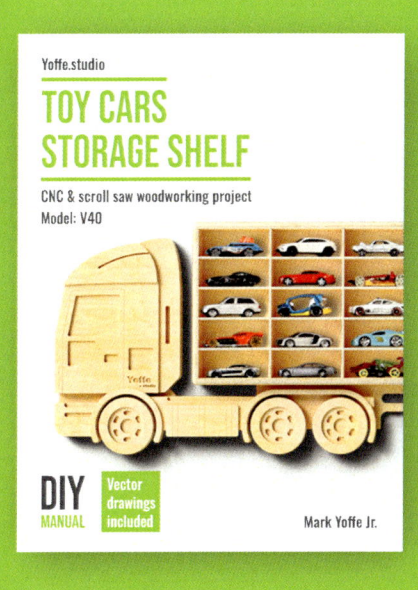

Model: H60

Toy cars extension storage shelf

Model: F60

Toy cars storage shelf

Model: V40

Toy cars storage shelf

Made in United States
Orlando, FL
12 January 2025